THE
Presence
OF ABSENCE

A Story About
Busyness, Brokenness, and Being Beloved

To Georgia with gratitude, :)

Linda Hoye

05/25/20

ALSO BY LINDA HOYE

Two Hearts: An Adoptee's Journey Through
Grief to Gratitude

LINDA HOYE

THE *Presence* OF ABSENCE

A Story About
Busyness, Brokenness, and Being Beloved

BENSON

The Presence of Absence: A Story About Busyness, Brokenness, and Being Beloved
By Linda Hoye

Benson Books
Kamloops, British Columbia

Contact the author at linda@lindahoye.com
www.lindahoye.com

ISBN (print): 978-0-9937303-0-6
ISBN (ebook): 978-0-9937303-1-3

Cover design and interior layout by Yvonne Parks at Pear Creative
PearCreative.ca

Dedication

For Laurinda and Michael

TABLE OF CONTENTS

PART 1
Busy

Chapter 1
SEARCHING

Here is your life. You might never have been, but you are, because the party wouldn't have been complete without you. Here is the world. Beautiful and terrible things will happen. Don't be afraid. I am with you. Nothing can ever separate us. It's for you I created the universe. I love you.

Frederick Buechner, *Wishful Thinking*

The late-August sunshine beats warm through the window of our Ford Escape. Gerry and I are taking a few days away from work to visit our son, Michael, in 100 Mile House, British Columbia, to celebrate his thirty-second birthday. We're making a stop along the way. Our journey takes us north, from Washington State through Chilliwack, British

Columbia, and I promised myself the next time we were in the area I'd find the place where my birth mom was buried.

It feels like we're always going. If I'm not on a plane, I'm on the highway. If we're not going somewhere, we're making plans to go somewhere. It's staying connected in the twenty-first century. It's the by-product of having means and opportunity to go places and do things my parents and grandparents couldn't have imagined. Family visits, writing conferences, appointments required while living with one foot in Canada and the other in the United States: all good and necessary things. But I long to nest like I could before the world got so small. Going keeps the undercurrent of grief I feel at having lost more than one family at bay. It gives me a sense of significance I don't otherwise have. But I'm growing weary.

Once I got up before dawn on Monday morning two or three weeks out of every month to begin the trek—either driving or flying, depending on the time of year—from Kamloops, British Columbia, to my office in Federal Way, Washington. Five-and-a-half hours door to door: that was my morning commute. With little else to do after hours but sit in a hotel room when I was in Washington, work was all-encompassing. When I was home in British Columbia I made quilts, served my church, cooked Sunday dinners for whichever of our kids showed up, and on evenings and weekends in the summer I sat on our sundeck overlooking a golf course and read good books. I cultivated a life. But, two-and-a-half years of this pace was enough, and we moved to Washington. I had enough of travelling and wanted to spend more time at home.

It was exciting—a new chapter—but when we crossed the border in our car loaded with personal papers and things we'd need before the moving truck arrived at our new home in a week's time, I didn't realize I was leaving something of myself behind: the ability to maintain a healthy balance. Even with the busyness of having a foot in two countries, life before the move had a rhythm that left room for creative activities and quiet reflection. Moving shook me. Leaving the city I called home for almost thirty years to go to a place familiar in terms of my work, but where I needed to craft a personal life, brought challenges. I needed to prove myself. I relied on competency and recognition at work and in extracurricular activities to stabilize me. Now, as a fiftyish-year-old woman I resent corporate and self-imposed demands keeping me in perpetual motion. Gerry and I talk about the future. We discuss options—where we'll live and what we'll do when we retire.

"We have to get out of here," I say when that kid on the noisy motorized go-cart takes one more lap around the block, or the *thuck-thucking* of a local news helicopter overhead disturbs our Sunday morning peace.

I come home cranky and spent at the end of the day and pour out my frustrations about work. We take short vacations, a few days at a time, to visit our family back in Canada and I try to unplug for a few days. It's too easy to check messages. And what can it hurt to email a reply—or two, or ten—when I'm doing nothing but sitting in the passenger seat of our car? I barely remember what it was like when "out of office" meant unplugged.

But it's more than minor irritants at home and restlessness at work making me dream of a little house on the prairie where I can tend a garden and take long, solitary walks along dusty range roads. Panic keeps me wide-eyed in the wee hours. I'm running out of time on this earth and wonder if the going and doing will give me a strong enough sense of significance so that I'll be able to relax one day. I lay awake at night with the gnawing sense they aren't.

Now, as we shake off the tension of having crossed the border into Canada and Gerry pulls onto the Trans Canada Highway from Sumas Way, he asks the question I've been asking myself all morning.

"How do you feel about seeing her grave?"

My husband's question is simple—the answer, far more complicated. How do I feel about a posthumous reunion with Mary, the woman who gave birth to me but severed connection with her daughter immediately?

It's a consolation prize. Every time I watch a scene in a TV show or movie depicting a mother-child reunion I feel the same way: robbed. I started searching for Mary when I was twenty-six-years-old—five months after my adoptive mom, Laura, died of a pulmonary embolism, and eighteen months after my adoptive dad, Ed, died of post-surgical complications. By then Mary had already been gone for six years.

I feel guilty, too. Even after all these years, there's still a twinge of guilt when I imagine what Ed and Laura would think of me poking around and trying to find the truth about my family of origin. They wouldn't understand my needing to know where I came from took nothing away from how much I loved them. They were my parents, period. But it would hurt them. They believed, like many adoptive parents in the late 1950s and beyond, the wide-eyed four-month-old baby the case worker gently placed in Laura's arms was a blank slate. Her heritage wasn't important. They would perceive my basic need to know as a failure on their part or rejection on mine.

"I don't feel one way or the other," I say, rummaging around in my purse for my phone. "It's just something I need to do."

And yes, that's true too.

I've thought about Mary all my life. From the beginning, when she was nameless and faceless, through the years I spent chipping out a place for myself in my family of origin, she has been on my mind. I gleaned second-hand insight into her character, learned about her (our) Mennonite heritage, and examined every snippet of information I could get for something to connect us, yet she remained elusive.

Over the course of the four years it took to write a memoir called *Two Hearts: An Adoptee's Journey Through Grief to Gratitude,* I learned to compartmentalize my adoption-related feelings as I processed my pain and made peace with it. When the book was published, I was strong with the fierceness that comes when you stake a claim on your truth and own all you have done and who you have been. I'd become adept at stuffing grief, guilt, and whatever else bubbled up back down because it hurt. And who wants to hurt? My intention in standing at Mary's grave is to tie a virtual bow around my adoption narrative. I've written the book, done the work, found the truth, and it is time to move on. With this act I intend to close the door on adoption.

I did some sleuthing before we left home and found records showing where Mary was buried. I pull out my phone and set the GPS to guide us there. Finding the graveyard is easy. Finding my birth mother proves to be more of a challenge.

———————

Mary was a quiet woman with a strabismus, giving her a slightly cross-eyed look. I read in my adoption file she felt like she had never "come first" with her family, her husband, or anyone else. She saw herself as the "black sheep." This is where my story begins.

For reasons I'll never know, my biological mom didn't see herself as precious and, as a result, wasn't able to hold others to account who didn't treat her as such. She longed for the best but struggled to believe she was worthy of it and was willing to accept less than she deserved. But she was beloved before, during, and after everything that happened to and because of her. Nothing could erase her position as beloved. If only she could have seen it. Our only hope in overcoming the brokenness we're all doing our best to stumble through life with is in believing we're beloved. But I'm getting ahead of myself.

In 1949, when she was thirty years old, Mary answered an advertisement in the *Western Producer* from a man seeking a wife. It wasn't an uncommon practice in those days on the Canadian prairies for a man to find a wife in that manner. John took Mary away from her Saskatchewan family to British Columbia to begin their married life, but it didn't turn out to be the fairy-tale ending she hoped for. John was abusive (Mary claimed he once tried to choke her to death), and they separated after a few months. They never divorced, neither did they ever reconcile.

With only an eighth-grade education and low self-esteem to boot, Mary saw few options. She supported herself working as a housekeeper for a series of unattached men. The relationship between her and some of those men crossed the line from employer–employee to something else.

She became pregnant the first time in 1952 and her oldest sister adopted her child—a son she named Donald. She became pregnant a second time two years later and kept this baby, another son, naming him Merlin. In the early spring of 1958, Mary answered an advertisement for a housekeeper in the home of a man named Francis—or Frank, as I've always thought of him.

Mary later described Frank as a tall, thin, lonely man, who was not especially good looking. Married, but separated from his wife and four children, he lived in a small house on his family's land. He was unkind, one could even say cruel. (Later, his daughter, my half-sister, described him that way to me: "He was mean." I heard stories of abuse, abandonment, and a man who took out his pain on those around him. It was difficult to learn about the character of my birth-father and sort through thoughts of what there was of him in me.) But Mary had no way of knowing that when she and four-year-old Merlin moved into his home. Mary and Frank's relationship crossed the line right away, but according to Mary, there was "no great love" between them. She left after a few months when Frank became violent. A man of low character, he slandered Mary to others in the same way he had slandered his wife and children to Mary. Mary sent a letter to Frank telling him she was pregnant and asking for financial help, but he never responded. He had already chosen to walk away from his responsibilities to the four children he had with his wife, so why would he do anything different now? Mary must have felt overwhelmed and alone.

Summer turned to fall, and Mary returned to Saskatchewan, but not to the care of her family. Winter blew in and, alone and under a shroud of secrecy, Mary delivered her third child—a daughter. That she had given birth to a baby girl this time made it all the harder to relinquish her to adoption. The doctor prescribed medication to help cope with her distress.

The language the court used in those days was not kind. A child welfare worker swore under oath she "apprehended the baby in court"[1] because she "believed the child was born out of wedlock and the mother was unwilling to maintain the child." The judge ruled I was "a neglected child within the meaning of the Child Welfare Act" and ordered me "committed to the care and custody of the Minister of Social Welfare and Rehabilitation permanently." A judge signed the Order of Committal and handed me off to the care of a foster mother.

After a few months the doctor recommended tests for me because of non-specific symptoms and I was hospitalized for a month (!) before being deemed healthy and "suitable for adoption." I was four months old when I joined my adoptive parents and Linda Louise Gunther became Linda Gail Brauer. Officials sealed the records about my pre-adoption truth and—poof!—it was as if Mary and I had never been connected at all.

Five years after she gave birth to me, Mary delivered another daughter in similar circumstances. She kept this sweet, blonde baby girl for a few months but ultimately felt she had no choice but to surrender baby Wendy to adoption too. I can't imagine Mary's grief.

Many years later I came into possession of a small trunk containing paraphernalia from my birth mother's short and sad life. Inside were photos of Donald, Merlin, and sweet baby, Wendy. She even saved Wendy's little pink hairbrushes. There were small tokens showing Mary treasured three children in her heart. The only thing was, she had given birth to four and regardless of the reason, whether or not I understood it, that absence still hurt.

———————

Gerry finds a shaded spot next to a tall and spreading tree on the side of the gravel roadway in the cemetery to park the Escape. The grass in the graveyard is dry and brown in the hot August sun. We climb out of the car and I lift out our Yorkshire Terrier, Maya. I carry her in my arms like a security blanket and head off in one direction while Gerry goes the other.

According to the cemetery index, my half-brother, Merlin, was buried here nine years ago when he died of pancreatic cancer, so I keep an eye on the newer markers as well as weathered and moss-covered ones I imagine Mary's twenty-seven-year-old one to be. Up and down, and back and forth I walk, now and then bending down to brush grass off a stone so I can read the inscription. *Where are you, Mother?* I mutter under my breath. It feels like I have always been searching. *Are you still hiding from me?*

I'm not sure how I'll respond to standing at Mary's grave and being near to her, in some manner, for the first—no, I suppose the second time. When I was in my early twenties, I stood at the graves of Laura and Ed feeling alone and lost as my world crashed down around me. They died eighteen months apart, and I was orphaned for a second time. I didn't know what to do, but I figured it out, and part of figuring it out turned out to be looking for my truth in the shadowy forms of Mary and Frank. I wasn't looking for parents, I was looking for something to anchor me. I was helpless, floating around like an astronaut in the black void of space, with no way to get back into the security of the rocket ship. I was looking for my past so I could figure out my future. But it was too late; I was already truly an orphan.

"Over here!" Gerry's call startles me from my inner musing.

"Did you find it?" I yell back and he beckons.

I take a deep breath and walk toward him, cuddling my little Yorkie tighter. When I get there, he points at the stone in front of him and I kneel to get a closer look. Merlin, not Mary's, name is inscribed on it. She must be nearby. I stand and step around the maze of nearby headstones, and Gerry does the same in the opposite direction. My throat tightens. *Where are you? Why do you elude me even now?*

It doesn't take long to cover the whole cemetery. Our search for a second grave is unsuccessful. We meet again at Merlin's headstone and I pull out my phone to take another look at the electronic document listing names and location coordinates of the graves. This time I notice something I hadn't seen before: the coordinates for Mary and Merlin's graves are the same—122-05. Maybe they refer to a general area and not a specific grave site. Gerry waits as I walk up and down rows, scrutinizing names on tombstones and comparing them to the coordinates on the list, desperate to find something to help me find my mother. My throat tightens further, my heart pounds, and I wrestle to accept we'll find nothing else today.

"They must be buried together."

I kneel and brush dust and grass from around the sides of my brother's headstone, looking for something to indicate the remains of two people are buried in this spot, but I find nothing. I can only assume Merlin was laid to rest in the same then-unmarked grave as our mother was years earlier and someone acknowledged him, but not Mary.

"We can phone the church later and see if we can get more information," Gerry suggests.

Yes, we can but I wanted an opportunity to stand at Mary's grave and to be certain, in a sense, we were both in the same place at the same time. Maybe that's happening now or maybe it isn't.

"I need a minute," I say.

I reach up and hand Maya to Gerry and, as he walks away, rest my palms on the grass. I've always hated it when someone tells me to breathe during a crisis—breathing isn't something I'm likely to forget to do—yet here I am reminding myself to inhale and exhale and the steadiness of my breath is keeping me from shattering. *How do you feel about* not *seeing her grave?*

I'm angry at Merlin. It's safer to be angry at my brother, the only one out of all of us she raised. Mary's sister once told me he was over-protective of her, now it seems to me he protects her even in death. But I can't deny I'm angry at Mary too. There's no reason for it, but my anger protects me from the more painful and familiar feelings of abandonment and rejection not finding her (or finding her?) pushed to the surface. She turned me away again. She kept me from being able to tell her I forgive her for something needing no forgiveness. Or maybe it's me I need to forgive, for choices I made that our separation partially explains but doesn't excuse. Instead, I'm coming away with more questions, and the most disquieting emptiness.

I rise, raw and vulnerable, and walk toward the car. Gerry wraps his arms around me and pulls me close. My throat burns. I will not cry. Instead, I latch the door on the pain that has surfaced. It's too dangerous. I always knew it.

Two weeks later, after some sleuthing, we learn Merlin's cremated remains were laid to rest in the same grave where our mother was buried. It bothers me their common resting place bears no reference to Mary and I think about purchasing a marker for her. The church says they will lay it if we do, and it seems ironic the forgotten daughter considers honouring her memory. But I don't get around to doing it, and I don't close the book on adoption either. Instead, I turn to my drug of choice to help me deal with the lingering pain.

Busyness is a two-fold saviour. It numbs my hurt and the fruit of it makes me feel significant in a world I experience through a filter of feeling abandoned and rejected.

Some wounds, like one inflicted by perceived or real rejection by one's mother, are too deep to heal completely. This is the grief I carry; we all have something. Every one of us has some wound that hurts, bleeds, and heals, and then some new injury rips the scab off so that it hurts, bleeds, and heals again and again. For me, in that deep place I keep safe and away from prying eyes, I ache over the loss of my first mother's love. It's probably something else for you, but that same ache and emptiness is there to some degree. We do our best to carry on despite it. Most of us work around it and become contributing members of society. Others succumb.

Relative to what someone else is asked to endure, perhaps our own momentary troubles are slight, and yet God doesn't deal in relativity like that. My pain is as real as yours, just as yours is as real as someone else's. We look at the big picture and say, "We are blessed," and, indeed, that is so. But we're not asked to minimize our individual pain. We all have different capacities for bearing burdens. We all carry a weight that, at times, feels too heavy, and we struggle to bear it.

When we break a bone or strain a muscle, we take prophylaxis to help us cope with the pain. To ignore the discomfort is to invite further damage and we heal faster when we're not in a constant state of hurt. Without rest, and taking the time to heal, our bodies can't do what they're designed for. So, we rest, take short-term medication, and, in time, recover and return to good health. Unless we don't.

Sometimes our bodies get addicted to the things meant to give us relief from pain in the short term, causing unintended damage to ourselves and those around us. It works the same whether it's physical or emotional pain.

I don't like feeling the way I do when I think about never having the opportunity of being held in the arms of my mother. I don't like how I'm hyper-vigilant in picking up nuances of rejection and abandonment from ordinary interactions. I don't like feeling the fear baby Linda must have sensed when her mother was no longer there. I don't like any of these things, so I self-medicate by going and doing. It's not the best choice but, like Mary, I struggle to see myself as beloved. I opened the lid by going to the cemetery and now I'm having trouble stuffing everything back inside. I need to get busy.

Chapter 2

MIND-NUMBING

Like so many ambitious people, I had developed a dependence on adrenaline. I could get so much done when my anxiety was in the red zone that I learned to live right on the edge of panic, in that optimum zone between alarm and collapse. It was my version of running hurdles and I was good at it. As long as I kept moving quickly, there was a great deal I did not have to feel.

Barbara Brown Taylor, *Leaving Church: A Memoir of Faith*

Sometimes, on Saturday afternoon after the lawn is mowed, and the laundry washed, dried, and put away, we pack up our cameras and go for a drive. There's always something undone in the back of my mind as we back our car out of the driveway: flower beds not weeded, emails not answered, meals to be prepared, or, in my role as the distribution editor for a review site, books to mail out. But a drive through farmland on the meandering Green Valley Road and a stop at Mosby's to buy fresh vegetables, or a visit to the Lake Wilderness Park in Maple Valley to walk the trails and take photos pushes the undone things to the back of my mind.

One Sunday afternoon we're at the Lake Meridian Park in Kent, Washington watching a smattering of people fish off the pier. The park is busy with adults trying to eke as much out of the day as they can, and with children and dogs who are oblivious to the constraint of time. We walk out on the pier and I lean over the railing to watch a flock of ducks. They glide across the surface of water clear enough to see their webbed feet paddling. I feel like one of those ducks. I'm doing my best to make the path I take appear effortless, like I'm in control, but the reality is I'm paddling furiously beneath the surface. I create gentle and minimal ripples, weaving through clusters of other ducks who appear equally serene on the surface, but my poor skinny duck legs are tired.

How many others feel the same way? We're so busy paddling under the surface, and working so hard to maintain a calm countenance, we barely see one another. We dare not confess our misgivings—to show weakness is to risk toppling the house of cards we've spent so much time building. What are we doing to ourselves? We need to work, and a fulfilling career is a gift, but twenty-four-hour-a-day availability and blurred lines between work and home life come with a cost. I'm starting to ask if it's one I want to continue to pay. This going and doing and giving the best of myself to a corporation to the point that I have little left over for myself is getting old.

I watch as one duck waddles out of the water onto the shore. He plops himself down in the shade as his less-colourful partner follows his direction. They appear to be resting but maybe their poor, skinny duck legs are burning and cramping as they fluff their feathers over them and settle down to rest. They're at risk here on the shore, more so than they are in the water, so maybe they're hyper-vigilant—a little outside their comfort zone and somewhat vulnerable to predators. I know the feeling. I'm tired, lonely, and afraid too. One day is the same as another. Rinse and repeat.

———————

I've been awake most of the night, my mind awhirl with work projects and deadlines, wondering how I'll get it all done. As usual, sleep comes right before my alarm goes off and I reach over and hit the snooze button. I have such good intentions about getting up earlier for prayer and meditation but I'm so tired. A few extra minutes of stolen sleep seems more important than anything else. The alarm buzzes for the third time and jars me awake. I give up and reach for my phone to see what's happened at work since I went to bed.

It starts before we realize it, this busyness propelling us forward through school and on into careers. It helps us find our place. It's not intrinsically bad. But sometimes something shifts and we lose sight of who we were *before*. Before ratings on performance reviews and promotions became our fix. Before the number of hours given to a corporation and the number of double-and triple-booked slots on our calendar defined our significance and we began to sneer surreptitiously at those who arrive and leave on time and don't work through their lunch breaks. Before the boundaries between our personal and professional lives blurred and busy became a badge of honour worn with pride. Before we lost the ability or desire to sit in silence and listen. We stop nurturing relationships and no longer practise our faith in the way we intend. Our creative selves shrivel like dried, crispy leaves in the fall. We feel empty but we're too busy to pay attention to the gnawing. It chafes, so we get busier to mask the pain.

Once, the workday ended around the time the supper hour began. We transitioned from work to home life, enjoyed an evening meal with those we loved, then a class, a walk in the park, or a visit with a friend. Sometimes we sat on the front step and watched twilight fall. Now, on those occasional nights when we force ourselves to leave the office at a reasonable time, we schedule activities in the hour or so we choose to be offline. Too often we don't have the energy for anything other than falling on the couch in front of the television where we numb ourselves watching *Survivor* when we're barely surviving, ourselves. Our email is out of control and our calendars run our lives. The workday never ends and, thanks to technology, we're always available. Depending on our circadian rhythm, we're working and emailing in the wee hours of the night or long before dawn—or both. We check email and voice mail when we're on vacation, despite what our out-of-office messages claim. It's understood we can't afford to be out of the loop. Something is flying through cyberspace at all hours and landing in our inboxes, requiring something from us. We're never caught up. We're never finished. We've always got capacity to add one more ball to the ones we're already juggling.

We tell ourselves it won't always be this way. One day we'll have time to focus on things to nourish our creative right brains. When things slow down, we'll nurture our faith practices and reconnect our relationships. We're too busy now taking care of the important and urgent Quadrant 1[2] things: crises and problems that, when they become our focus, lead to burnout. In the elusive *someday* we'll take time for Quadrant 2: strategic planning and relationship building; we know this is where the value lies, if only we had time to devote to it. Before we realize what's happening, we veer off course and head in a direction we never intended.

I scroll through my unread emails. There's nothing that can't wait so I stumble out of bed toward the bathroom. I lean in toward the mirror where tired, empty eyes stare back at me and wonder if I'm selling my soul for the sake of a corporation.

Soon, fresh from the shower and with a towel wrapped around me, I flick on the radio and pull out my makeup tray. There's more news about the latest financial crisis, political turmoil, and natural and unnatural disasters. While I apply minimal makeup and blow dry my hair, I go through the list of things I need to do when I get to the office to prepare for my first meeting of the day. I move through my morning routine like an automaton. And there's that pressure in my chest again.

I remember something and reach for my phone.

You have one saved message. Press 1 to listen to your saved message.

1.

Hi, Grandma. It's Makiya. I want to Skype.

My two-year-old granddaughter's sweet voice makes me smile.

Press 9 to save your message.

9.

———————

Dried and colourless lilac blossoms tell me time has passed. I haven't taken time to snip a few sprigs of the fragrant purple flowers that once lined the front yard of my adoptive grandmother, Belle's, house and put them in a vase on my desk. Someone brought a bouquet into the office, and I made a mental note to go into our backyard and cut some for myself. Wasn't that yesterday? Now it's too late.

Last year, we bought a four-foot-by-four-foot raised garden bed, and I dropped tiny seeds in trenches and tended growing seedlings. It produced enough lettuce, radishes, and carrots for salads that I sprinkled pretty blue borage flowers on top of. As I tended my garden, I remembered cardboard boxes filled with green beans and potatoes we brought back from the farm to my grandma's house in the back of my uncle's pickup truck, the earthy taste of beet relish slathered on a thick slice of homemade white bread, and crocks of vinegar-sweet bread and butter pickles. Homesickness for something that was mine ever-so-briefly took hold.

I spend Saturday mornings with cups of coffee and worn copies of Mother Earth News magazine. I click around the "interweb" seeking information for the simple life I imagine, learning about succession planting, composting, and cut-and-come-again lettuce. Gerry buys, and sets up, a little plastic-covered greenhouse in which I can start plants. I put a ceramic chicken near the door and a metal goat on the other side and create a little farm right in my back yard.

The lilacs are finished blooming, but gardening season is beginning. This year we enlarged my little garden and I will plant peas, pole beans, beets, and spaghetti squash—and the latest trendy vegetable everyone is talking about, kale—in addition to salad vegetables. The garden invites me to pay attention. It draws me to take notice of day-by-day growth and invites me to linger. I scan the soil for signs of life when I come home from work and snip baby lettuce leaves to toss with a light vinaigrette to feed us. I drop seeds in pots in the greenhouse and tuck tiny seedlings in big flowerpots next to the pergola. I don't know much about what I'm doing but I'm hungry to learn. The garden reminds me of what it's like to take care of something. It, and the sunny southern exposure at the side of the house where we grow tomatoes, represents another way of living. I harvest more than vegetables from the little plot. Peace of mind is what I'm learning to grow.

––––––––––––

"Linda!" Gerry pokes his head out the sliding glass door leading from the kitchen to the backyard. "Come and see this."

I'm busy. I've just arrived home from work and am in the backyard watering and dead-heading petunias before I start dinner. It's a moment of quiet I look forward to after spending most of the day in my office, but I do my best to hide my annoyance at the interruption. I put the hose down and follow him in and through the house, and out the front door.

"Look," he points to the ground beside the house. Something must be wrong with my clematis. It hasn't been doing well and my stomach clenches at the thought of insects, or an animal, harming it further.

"What?"

My words are sharp. I can't see any damage to the plant and now I'm growing irritated by the interruption.

"Down there. Look."

I bend down and there it is: a tiny green frog, less than two inches long, tucked in the corner of the flower bed. I would never have seen it. In my single-minded way of rushing from one task to the next, I would have walked right past it when I came to the front yard to water these flowers. Gerry had pointed out a similar little frog sitting on the leaf of my squash plant on Saturday. I tried to photograph it but it hopped away before I could get my camera. He's giving me another opportunity.

"How did you ever see him there?" I ask.

I know the answer even as I lay down on the ground to get as close to it—without scaring it—as I can. My husband doesn't rush and hurry like I do. He takes his time and appreciates what's in front of him in every moment. When we were first married, I loved the fact he took time to observe the stars at night and appreciate the beauty of the moon's phases. Even now, he calls me out at night to look up in the sky sometimes.

"It's the moon," I say. "I've seen it before."

Then I hurry back to whatever I was busy with before the interruption. I tell him he'll live forever thanks to his easygoing manner, and I'll expire at my desk while on a conference call.

I stay on the ground and watch the frog, not even thinking about going to get my camera. A tear forms in the corner of my eye. I dismiss it with a swipe. Why can't I slow down? Why can't I walk the talk of appreciating the things I read about in magazines and on the simple living blogs I follow? What's wrong with me? If I don't change something, I'll continue to miss delights like the gift of this simple tiny green frog on a summer afternoon. And maybe I *will* die at my desk while I'm on a conference call.

———————

It's mid-August and summer has arrived in the Pacific Northwest. The forecast is for a stretch of sunny days, with temperatures reaching the high 80s and maybe—if we're lucky—the low to mid 90s. Gerry and I are among the minority in our neighbourhood with our love of the heat. Our neighbours seek refuge in air-conditioned homes and shake their heads when we tell them how much we enjoy the hot weather. They struggle to believe us when we tell them we come from an arid and hot-in-the-summer place in Canada. Except for the neighbour behind us who sits on his patio and has loud telephone conversations (we know far more about his life than we wish), we're the only ones who spend most of the time we're at home outside in the yard.

I sip from the ever-present glass of water I keep at my desk and open my email, hoping to clear a handful of messages in the few minutes I have between meetings. I accept new meeting requests, reschedule others, and watch the few blank spots in my calendar fill with items marked *Urgent!* and *Important!* The invitations are always accompanied with a note of apology: "This is the only time I could find and we need to pull together on this issue. Sorry." I understand. I do the same thing to other people. I'm a business analyst. I lead a team of other business analysts and manage projects. I love the work but, increasingly, it's sucking the life from me.

I continue to scroll, scanning the columns with the sender's name and subject lines, looking for emails I can delete without reading. Too many subject lines begin with *FW:* indicating email trails that have gone back and forth and have grown to a behemoth requiring another meeting to sort out, likely resulting in more tasks being added to my already-full project plan. I delete all but the most recent of the bunch, saving it to read later. There's an email from Gerry with no subject line and one sentence in the body: *Meet you on the patio at 5.*

I send a quick reply: *Yes!! See you soon!*

———————

A co-worker stops me on my way to the parking lot. He wants to talk about projects and priorities and all I can think about is every minute I spend talking to him is a minute I'm not on my patio squeezing as much as I can from the limited amount of free time I have coinciding with the Pacific Northwest sunshine. I do my best not to appear rude as I extricate myself from the conversation, promising to follow up in the morning.

I pull out onto Highway 18 and my mind switches from work to home mode. What should I make for supper?

Did I remember to take dog food out of the freezer before I left this morning? I have to get back on email when I get home. When I checked earlier, I saw something I need to tend to for my writing group. I must remember to water the bedding plants I picked up on the weekend.

Maya greets me as soon as I open the door. There's nothing like the enthusiastic welcome of a little wiggling Yorkie tail to make you happy to be home. I give her a treat and head for the stairs leading up to the bedroom to shed my work clothes and change into something more relaxed for patio time. By the time I return, clad in capri pants and a t-shirt, Maya is at the sliding glass door, as eager as I am to enjoy the rest of the sunny day outside. Gerry walks in while I'm racing around the room gathering my reading glasses, book, and a few magazines.

"Hurry! The sun's still shining! Get changed and let's go outside," I urge.

When I've got my supplies assembled, I shout upstairs where Gerry hasn't yet returned from changing his clothes. "Come on! Let's go!"

I'm so accustomed to living in Quadrant 1 I've learned to slot down-time there too.

––––––––––––

With one bare pedicure-pretty foot tucked underneath me and the other touching the surface of the patio, the lawn swing sways, and I relax. I'm reading the latest *Maclean's* magazine to keep abreast of what's happening in Canada and sipping a second glass of cold chardonnay. Out of the corner of my eye, I see Gerry put his book down and reach for his t-shirt. I sense his restlessness and groan inwardly, I'm not ready to break the spell of patio time.

"I think I'll go in and catch the news," he says, reaching for his empty wine glass.

"Are you getting hungry?" I know the answer. I wish I didn't.

"Getting there."

I groan and toss my head back in an exaggerated display of angst at the thought of having to go in the house and pull together supper while it's still warm outside.

"When we retire, I'm going to sit outside in the sunshine for as long as I want," I declare.

I try to plan ahead, when patio weather is in the forecast, by preparing an assortment of salads, pre-cut fruit, vegetables, cheese, and cold cuts we can pull out for a light supper on summer evenings. Other times, I cook a large meal on the weekend so we'll have leftovers for weeknights. This time, I've been too busy to be proactive.

"If I were a millionaire, I'd have a cook and never make supper ever again." I continue my sorry tale of woe. "I'd sit outside until it was dark. Half an hour more, okay? I'll finish reading this magazine, then I'll come in and make dinner."

Gerry smiles as he rises from his chair. As usual, he's in no hurry. He'll go in the house and pour a few more peanuts into his bowl to tide him over a little longer while I continue the work of relaxing.

A few days later something happens that gets my attention.

———————

"Go to the office and get my computer," I plead with my husband from my hospital bed.

I resigned myself to staying another night for further tests after they threatened (at least that's how I perceived it) my insurance carrier wouldn't look favourably on leaving against medical advice. I'm trapped, but the fact remains there's still work needing to be done. The pressure in my chest doesn't deter me from my sense of responsibility. Gerry refuses (thank goodness!) and I've no choice but to unplug. Imprisoned, I continue to worry about my projects and lament the fact I'm missing the late-September warm weather—likely the last of the season. Patio days are slipping through my fingers. There's that panic again and the fear I'm running out of time.

I'm released after two days, my heart given the all-clear and stress deemed to be the culprit. The news is good and not so good. Good, because it's not something more serious. Not so good, because there's no pill or surgical procedure to fix the pressure in my chest. I promise to manage stress better. I work on a beautiful campus and there's no reason I can't take a walk through the park-like paths at lunchtime. I promise I'll leave the office on time. By six o'clock. Honest.

———————

It's dark and cool at six thirty in the morning when I climb out of my car, toss my keys into my purse, and fling it over my shoulder. I grab my tote bag from the back seat and my coffee cup from the front. The short walk from my car to the office building where I work is pretty. The campus is a haven tucked between interstates filled with trees and green space. Ivy grows on the walls of the award-winning building, making it blend into the landscape. There's a large pond next to it where geese nest in the spring.

I hurry across the parking lot, my mind already on projects and meetings and the email messages I read when I woke up. As I get close to the office door, I loop the handle of my tote bag over my left arm and transfer my coffee to my right hand, allowing me to reach for the security badge attached to a lanyard around my neck in a practised move I do without thinking every morning.

"I'll get that door for you. You've got your hands full."

I turn and see a young man who sits in a cubicle down the hall from me walking about twenty feet behind. I hadn't even realized he was there. My first instinct is to brush off his offer to help—*it's okay, I've got it*—but I choke back the words as I realize it would be rude to refuse his kindness. I do it all the time—refuse help and insist on relying on my own strength. Now it strikes me people might perceive my independence as impolite. So often I miss interacting with someone and I insist on doing it myself. I'm trying to let the lesson of my recent hospital stay teach me a better way.

"Thank you!" I smile, stepping to the side to allow him to use his security badge to unlock the door and pull it open. I walk through the door in front of him, wish him a good day, and we go our separate ways. How hard was that?

––––––––––––––––

I sign up for a once-a-week exercise class after work—an easy transition from the workday to an evening at home, forcing me to get out of the office on time. I arrive home in a more relaxed state. Gerry suggests I go more than once a week.

One evening after class, I turn the corner of the on-ramp from Auburn toward Highway 18 and am greeted by a snaking line of red taillights stretching as far as I can see. I ease into the right lane, nod to the kind driver who let me into the red-light parade, and switch on my CD player. I bought a new Sarah Brightman album when I was on the way to Canada to attend an adoption workshop during the weekend. I stopped to do some shopping at the outlet mall and heard the most beautiful music playing in a shop. When I asked the clerk who it was, she pointed it out to me on the shelf, and I picked up a copy immediately.

I inch along with the rest of the traffic wondering what's caused the delay. I grow impatient, frustrated that my post-class sense of mellow is fading, and think about turning on the radio to see if I can get a traffic report. But as Sarah sings something shifts. If I turn the radio on and find the cause of the traffic incident, I won't get through it any faster. Why not just listen to the music? I put my head back on the headrest, keeping my eyes on the red taillights, and enjoy the extra solitary minutes. The inconvenience turns into a blessing and I arrive home relaxed, happy, and at peace. I take note and promise to remember this lesson.

Gerry and I decided photography would make a good joint retirement hobby. We bought new Canon cameras and signed up for two classes at the local college: one on technique, the other on the art of photography. I took notes week after week as my brain twisted, and I tried to understand the exposure triangle and the relationship between aperture, ISO, and shutter speed. I'm told I have to understand these things before the buttons and dials on my fancy camera will make sense. I wonder what I've gotten myself into. We're given prompts at the end of each class to play with in the coming week and are invited to send two photos to the instructor before we meet again. He displays them on the screen in front of the class for critique. I agonize week after week over this part.

Early in the morning, when the light is best, I go outside in my pyjamas. I shoot images of wisteria and columbine in the backyard. I spritz water from a bottle on ferns and get down on the ground to take photos. One week, the prompt is abstract, and it threatens to send me over the edge of sanity. I look for inspiration in the shower and later take photos of water drops on the tempered glass door. I set up an elaborate tower of wine glasses filled with water, olive oil, and food colouring on top of a mirror and take top-down photos. I pour pistachios into a bowl and shoot close-ups. I try everything I can think of to kick my creative right brain into gear, but it's atrophied. Creativity hurts. Finally, I come up with something barely better than nothing and send it to the instructor right before class.

I don't realize it, but my first feeble attempts at creativity are firing up synapses in my brain that haven't been sparking as a result of prolonged stress. I'm awakening a part of myself that's been stagnant. My photography stinks, but what's happening inside is the start of something beautiful.

I attended a writing conference in Austin, Texas. In some sessions we wrote, in others we listened. I came away from all of them inspired. The lecture-type sessions were easiest; I struggled to scribble down words in the ones requiring participation. As with photography, the creative part of my brain I needed to tap into to write wasn't firing as I needed it to.

During an afternoon break I went outside and stretched downward with my palms flat on the brown earth in the hotel courtyard. It's my instinct to do so after I've been cooped up indoors for too long—maybe a subconscious attempt to draw energy from the earth and return to who I am. I rested my hands on the surface of a teak table beside the swimming pool. Though the aged timber no longer lives I could feel the same energy in the warm, weathered wood as when I was palms-down on the ground. I thought about life and the absence of life; the contrast between earth, the wood, the cold steel of the chain-link fence, and the plastic roughness of the life preserver hanging on it. It was easy to see the difference between what was alive and what wasn't. It's more challenging back home when I'm caught up in busyness.

Fresh from a session where the presenter talked about paying attention to sensual details to set a scene, I pondered some things I know for certain. I need to be silent to hear truth the loudest. There are lessons in the chirp of a red-winged blackbird or the call of a blue jay who drops by to snack at one of the feeders in my yard. If I stand outside at 3 a.m. and breathe sweet night air, feeling it brush across my bare skin as I listen to frogs and crickets, I will hear a divine whisper. The delicate scent of lilac blossoms takes me home. Pink gladioli swaying in the breeze remind me of my mom. I'm meant to go barefoot; covering my feet with obligatory black trouser socks and constraining dress shoes every morning stifles me. Constant exposure to the cold and lifeless interior of an office building suffocates my creative right brain. Ficus trees and peace lilies in the corridors are not reasonable facsimiles for the outdoors. The most important things are not things. I've lost touch with the truth.

———————

One morning, I was driving down the interstate toward my office when I passed a billboard with an image of palm trees, turquoise water, and a couple relaxing in lounge chairs on a sandy beach. A caption—*The Good Life*—was scrawled across the bottom of the billboard and, in smaller letters, the name of the financial planning business it advertised. Gerry and I often escape to warmer destinations in the dead of winter—at least we did before the grandchildren arrived and altered our vacation plans. There's no doubt it's a slice of the good life. But if that's the good life, what does it say about everyday life? Is it the not-so-good life? The less-than-perfect life? The covetous-not-content life?

Harvesting and chopping vegetables for dinner, folding laundry, sharing a laugh with Gerry, sitting in my office getting ready for a meeting, writing in my home office, hugging my grandchildren, crying tears of frustration, sitting on the couch with my neck massager trying to ease the pain in my shoulders. *This*, right now. The extraordinary moments of an ordinary life. Aren't these the good life too? Stress, my nemesis and sleep stealer tries to rob me of it but deep down inside I know the tapestry of a life well lived is woven with ordinary God-glorifying moments. Yet I continue to seek significance and purpose *out there* despite knowing it's somehow *right here* in ordinary time.

———————

Busyness isn't the problem. My need to numb is the problem. I'm finally starting to see it. It's manifested in my hunger to exceed expectations and looks like a calendar full of meetings and conference calls and volunteer things holding my attention from the first waking moment when I reach for my smartphone to that last check of email before I turn out the light and fall into bed exhausted and with the help of a sleeping pill. I continue to eat antacid and ignore the heaviness in my chest. I forget my intention to take lunchtime walks on the campus. I come to the end of the year with a plethora of unused vacation days I burn by taking Fridays off. But I'm never really "off." I take conference calls, come to the office for meetings, and I always stay on top of email. I have a glass or two—occasionally three— of chardonnay at the end of the day to wind down. I hang a photograph of my granddaughter on the wall in my home office with a caption: *Take care of this girl's grandma.* A low-grade dissatisfaction burns. I'm tired of having little left over for myself.

One late-September afternoon, on the way home from spending a few days visiting our kids and grandkids in Calgary, we pass through Kamloops, the Canadian city we left behind when we moved to Washington State. We've been talking about the future, making plans to repatriate, and considering where to put down new roots. A farm in Saskatchewan looked attractive for a while until we got practical and thought about the distance it was away from our grandchildren and wondered at the wisdom of retiring to a place and a lifestyle most retire from. On this trip, we toured houses in bedroom communities near Calgary, but nothing spoke to us. Tears fell from my eyes as we got on the Trans Canada Highway and drove away from the city. The Rocky Mountains loomed in the distance and I felt my dream of returning to live in the prairies fall away.

Now, we're sitting in the sunshine in a park in Kamloops. A breeze blows barely enough that we have to weigh the paper wrappings of our sandwiches down with water bottles. I hear a faint whisper. *Stay.* I decide to see where it leads.

"What would you think about returning to Kamloops?"

We've talked about many places, but Kamloops wasn't one of them. Gerry saw our retirement as an opportunity to go somewhere new and to try something different. Why waste an opportunity like this by returning to the place we had already called home for over thirty years? He tilts his head back, takes a long drink from the water bottle, and then looks around.

The leaves on the trees in the park are starting to change colour. A young mom pushing a jogging stroller trots down the River's Trail. Overhead, a V of Canada geese heading south honk farewell. An older couple walks hand-in-hand toward the waterfront—and maybe that's what nudges him off the fence. He smiles, almost begrudgingly, as if it's something he considered but hasn't yet spoken aloud.

"It's home," he concedes.

———————

When I turned fifty, we made a five-year-plan, agreeing a reduced pension was an acceptable price to pay for the gift of time. We adjust our plan—now a one-year-plan—to return to Kamloops. I create a paper chain with a link for every month left before my retirement-eligible fifty-fifth birthday and hang it in my office: a visual reminder of time passing and a second act waiting. At work, my team refers to me as a "short-timer" as I start handing off projects. I sort through my desk filled with twenty-five years worth of paperwork and assorted ephemera, keeping trinkets I imagine tossing into a drawer in our new home in Canada for the grandkids to find. I keep cards and plaques and personal notes and read a quarter-century worth of performance reviews one last time before tossing them in a bin in the supply room to be shredded.

I'm walking away from a satisfying and lucrative career that has provided ample opportunity for professional and personal growth. It's been a good run, but I'm looking forward to not feeling over-extended all the time. I'm walking toward a simple life back in Canada with time for family, creativity, and the opportunity to give the best of myself to different things. No more meetings. No more conference calls—or risk of dying at my desk while on one. I'll devote my energy to the thing I've loved since I was nine years old when I wrote and illustrated my first little book: writing. I already have the outline of a novel waiting to be fleshed out. Thanks to the classes Gerry and I took, I understand enough of the basics of photography that I can continue to hone the craft on my own. And Kamloops is a gardener's paradise. There's more than enough to keep me occupied, but not busy, in retirement.

On my birthday, Gerry delivers a massive bouquet of fifty-five long-stemmed roses to my office and two important emails stand out amid the glut of business ones I receive. The community garden coordinator in Kamloops confirms the availability of a plot, and the movers confirm our dates.

I obsess about a plethora of details, as we prepare to retire, relocate, and repatriate. One of these alone requires copious amounts of planning and organization—together they are crazy-making. A black Moleskine notebook filled with lists, lists within lists, and clipped-together stacks of paper-work—one for the country we're leaving, the other for the one we're returning to—are my constant companions so I'm able to tend to things that come up on the fly.

I pause as I'm heading out the door on my way to work one morning. Am I forgetting something?

"We must be getting closer," I say to Gerry, who looks up from his morning reading. "I don't think I have any tasks to give you today."

Then it's time. Fist bump! It's our last Friday. I kiss my husband goodbye and head out into an unexpectedly snowy February morning on the last Friday I'll spend in the office. Next week there will be retirement celebrations, the movers will come to finish packing and load the truck. In a little over a week, we'll cross the border and head toward our new home in Canada. The anticipation terrifies me.

One night I'm fretting over a detail about something as we're getting ready for bed.

"This is getting on my last nerve."

"Don't worry, Linda. Your nerves will grow back when we get to Canada," Gerry predicts.

I expect he's right. When the countless details are tended to and we're settled back in Kamloops, things will be different.

"Once we get there, I'll never use the word *busy* to describe my life again. I'm done with being busy."

Chapter 3

THE PRESENCE
OF ABSENCE

If you're silent for a long time, people just arrive in your mind.

Alice Walker

Pediculous. Adjective. Infested with lice: lousy.

With my chin resting in my hand, I stare at the page on my word-of-the-day desk calendar. I had good intentions when I bought it. Anticipating a new year and a new post-career life, I imagined myself at my desk every morning tapping out sentences using the word *de jour*. It has been months since we moved. I've yet to tap out anything. Who am I without a business card or a job title? That's the question I ponder as I alternate glances between the nagging calendar and the snow-covered hills on the other side of the ridge. How do I carve out a new niche?

The ridge we now live on overlooks a valley where the South Thompson River joins the North Thompson River in a confluence flowing into the Kamloops Lake. Opposite Juniper Ridge, our subdivision, is an ever-changing-with-the-seasons ridge where desert-like hills and hoodoos turn from winter white to spring green and summer brown. The shadows in the silt change from hour to hour and season to season. It's almost distracting in its beauty.

But I miss sharing stories with the women in my writing group in Washington. I miss straining to see the goats when we drive down the hill from our neighbour-hood. I miss driving up Highway 18 toward Covington, grabbing a Frappuccino, and going for a pedicure at my favourite place. Retiring, relocating, and repatriating all at the same time is like starting over again—no, not *like*, it *is* starting over again.

Everyone I know who's left the workforce says they're living their post-career best life. They're all busy doing things they love and don't know how they found time to work. Retirement exceeds their expectations. One day I run into a man who says of his wife she "failed retirement" and returned to part-time work. I don't mention I've been considering doing the same thing. I hear rumblings of someone who lost themselves after they got the mythical golden handshake and died. I don't want to follow any of these examples. I want to carve out my own path.

Once I dreamed of spending an entire day reading a book, or sitting in the park and writing, but the thought of doing either makes me feel guilty—and lazy. When I was fresh out of school and short on experience, they encouraged us to list hobbies on our resumes to show how well-rounded we were. It didn't seem enough to say reading and writing so I padded my resume and said I enjoyed hiking. I didn't enjoy hiking (I enjoy it even less now that Gerry has taken it up and I see how gruelling it can be) but it seemed more acceptable than reading or writing and more believable than skiing or dancing. Even then I felt an unspoken pressure to be *more*. To want little more than to take advantage of time to read and write seems insufficient.

I slept better than I had for years once we were settled in our new home. It was a homecoming, returning to the city that was ours for thirty-years before we moved away, but it was also like waking up from a seven-year-long nap. I felt like Marty McFly in the *Back to the Future* movies when I went out. There was no Fred Meyer, but Safeway looked the same as the one I shopped at in Washington. That familiarity was comforting when we moved to the United States and it's the same in reverse now. I recognized people in stores and was startled at how they had changed until I remembered I've changed, and aged, in seven years too.

I know we're back in Canada because everything is labeled in both English and French. Every English-speaking kid growing up in Canada learns rudimentary French reading the back of cereal boxes and other packaging. I can't speak the language, but the words on the back of a pink box of bubble bath is burned in my mind from childhood. *Bain du mousse nettoyant pour les enfants.* Bubble bath for kids. The ear worm accompanies me as I walk up and down the aisles at the grocery store. Everything's more expensive than it was in Washington, but I can buy J-Cloths, China Lily Soy Sauce, and Crispy Crunch candy bars again. I'm confused when the woman at the check-out tells me I can pay for my purchase by swiping my debit card, inserting the chip end, or tapping. It reminds me of when I asked if I could use Interac in Washington and was met with a blank stare by the salesclerk.

The same big box stores bookend the biggest shopping mall. They're renovated and departments have moved but the familiar bones are still intact. I felt cool carrying my brand-new flip phone with me before we moved. Now everyone walks around the mall, head down and thumb scrolling. I listen to a radio talk show one day where they mention commonplace technical things that were taking off when we left Canada in 2007: smartphones, Netflix, Facebook, Twitter. No wonder I feel like the world tilted on its axis while we were gone.

I didn't fall back into the same space I occupied before we left. Either the shape of that round hole changed or my square-peg self no longer fit. We reconnected with old friends and met new people. I wished I could hand new acquaintances a copy of my resume to let them know I used to be someone. Once I was a business analyst. I led a team of human resource systems analysts working on cross-functional teams implementing corporate strategies of varying sizes and complexity. I started and facilitated a writing group. I took part in panel discussions at conferences about adoption and writing. I was on the board of an international writing organization. *Retired*, just isn't enough. I want to be seen, significant, and rooted, but I'm in an uncomfortable in-between place.

I became irritable. I couldn't stand myself, and I don't know how Gerry stood me either. I struggled to focus on the most quotidian things. It's like the customs officer seized my decision-making ability along with the contraband apple he found when he searched our vehicle before we crossed the border into Canada. Either that or I used up my decision-making quota during the retiring/relocating process. Choosing curtains and rods and deciding how to hang them, decisions about décor and appliances and new light fixtures, all paralyzed me and made me cranky. Without the protective shelter of I'm-too-busy-for-that-so-you-choose, I was pushed to make decisions on things I cared little about. I consulted websites and magazines and made unenthused choices.

Once I suggested to a co-worker contemplating retirement around the same time I was, that we needed to retire *to* something as opposed to *from* something. I was retiring to write. Having cut my teeth writing *Two Hearts*, I looked forward to being freed up from corporate responsibilities and sinking my teeth into something new. I imagined spending my days wrangling words in my home office, starting another writing group, and spending afternoons exploring and taking photos with Gerry. Once we got here, I couldn't seem to plant myself in my chair long enough to do anything. I dabbled with my camera and created images of calm that betrayed my anxiety.

I sit at my desk on mornings like this with my brain twisting, trying to write something but coming up with nothing. Maybe walking away from the corporate world was a mistake. Maybe the fantasy I entertained about living a slower and simpler life was nothing but a foolish dream. Would the better choice have been to keep going and doing for as long as I could to muffle the whispers reminding me of something I'll never have? I envy those who, at my age, still have the gift of a mother to talk to. On one hand I barely remember what it was like, on the other, I never knew.

Spring arrives, bringing an opportunity to get busy and a reason to stop ruminating on the mucky things that grow when my mind has too much time to think. As soon as the frost is out of the ground, I go to my new community garden plot and plant peas. I draw out an overall garden plan, paying attention to things I learned during my pre-retirement research about companion planting and each plant's individual sunlight and water requirements. I buy case after case of mason jars and stock up on freezer bags.

No longer defined by the title of "business analyst" and with no projects to plan and execute, I take on the mantle of CEO and project planner of my garden and kitchen. I realize, in the throes of meeting self-imposed deadlines on projects of my own choosing, I've traded one thing for another—retirement hobbies have turned into an obsession, and I can't seem to slow down.

By late August my kitchen hasn't been clean in months. Since the harvest began, an ever-changing array of garden-fresh produce covered my countertop starting with the first sweet spinach and radishes, then peas, Swiss chard, kale, scallions, beets, carrots, squash, onions, tomatoes, and cucumbers. The assortment varied from day to day and it ordered my steps. An endless parade of mason jars, lids, and rings appeared alongside the produce and almost every day involved me preserving something in jars or blanching and tucking away freezer bags full of vegetables. I stopped putting my canning paraphernalia away, sacrificing a tidy kitchen for the efficiency of having everything handy for almost-daily canning activities. Besides the standard jams, pickles, and relishes, I preserved Moroccan lemons, made cough syrup using peppermint from my garden, and canned watermelon rind pickles. When the cucumbers kept coming and I tired of making pickles and relish, I sliced them and put them in the dehydrator for snacks.

I preserve food like our ability to survive depends on it. I browse recipes looking for inspiration beyond the standard canned goods while enjoying early morning coffee in bed. Most mornings, I've got a plan in place before I set foot in the kitchen. I'm unapologetic for the mess I leave in my wake.

"This is a working kitchen," I say, as if my full-time job is growing and preserving food and I join the ranks of those post-career folk who don't know how they found time to work.

The shelves in the basement continue to fill with mason jars full of food and I post pictures on social media to prove how accomplished I am. But the gnawing remains. It's not enough. It's never enough.

One morning, I wrap the ties of my black apron around my waist and tie them in the front while inspecting jars of canned tomatoes I left on a towel on the countertop overnight. I remove rings, test seals, wipe and label the jars, make notations on a canning inventory sheet, and take a half dozen trips downstairs to where I line them up in organized and satisfying rows on a shelf. I stand back and admire the increasing bounty for a few precious moments before turning off the light and heading back upstairs.

There, I swirl water in white ramekins where tiny tomato seeds ferment on my windowsill. The seeds have separated from the gelatinous mass protecting them so I fish them out and lay them out on a paper towel next to the almost-dried bell pepper seeds. I inspect plates of drying herbs—basil, thyme, oregano, parsley, mint, and chives—and make a note to myself to sit down at the table later and pull the tiny dried thyme leaves from their stems and add them to the jar of dried herb.

One summer, almost forty years ago, I grew herbs for tea and potpourri in a wagon wheel garden I planted in my backyard. I've come full circle from that barefoot young woman who tended plants. She was doing her best to play the role of consolation prize as she mixed herb tea and scented potpourri. Now, I grab a pair of kitchen scissors and head outside to snip chamomile, still—after all these years—wearing the uncomfortable sense I should never have been born.

By midmorning I've harvested herbs and have six quarts of tomatoes processing in the pressure canner. Next to the sink on a towel, twenty clean pint jars sit waiting to be filled with vegetable soup. The house is heating up. When I was younger, in the days before I had the luxury of air conditioning, I fried chicken and boiled potatoes for salad early in the morning so the house would stay cool in the heat of the Kamloops afternoon. These days, I let the house get hot for the sake of preserving both food and my mental health. My back hurts and the tender spot between the third and fourth toes on my right foot burns like someone drove a red-hot poker through it. I tilt the blind on the east-facing window above the kitchen sink to keep the morning sun from shining in my eyes. It's dead quiet, save for the hissing of the pressure canner.

There's something bittersweet about making pickles. The tangy smell of boiling vinegar permeates the kitchen and reminds me of crocks filled with sweet mixed pickles in the storage room under the stairs in the house I grew up in. It opens the door to memories. I imagine sitting in my place at our yellow Formica kitchen table munching an egg salad sandwich and plucking a green onion from a glass in the middle of the table to dip in a hill of salt on the side of my plate. I ate quickly so I could go back outside and play with neighbourhood kids I'd known for as long as I could remember.

Debbie Green and I played make-believe in our back-yards in every one of the four seasons. We made forts, acted out stories, and coerced our younger siblings to join us in playing school. At the neighbourhood park we played on equipment long since banned for safety reasons. Maybe it was once, or maybe I directed variations of the same vignette ten times because the memory is so clear: Debbie was the mother and I was the daughter being embraced and welcomed home after a long and unexplained absence. Reunion games. I'm fifty-five years old and packing cucumbers in a mason jar when I realize I birthed the vignette out of a desire I wasn't able to articulate: to reunite with my first mother.

I think about my adoptive grandmother, Laura's mom, Belle, as I work. A hunched-back woman who has been dead for half a century, Belle already seemed old in photographs taken at my first Christmas though she was only sixty-three. When her youngest child was three-months old, her husband, Tenor, died from pneumonia leaving her with three children to raise by herself. The lion's share of parenting fell to Belle, but she leaned on Tenor's extended family who built a small house for her on the property next to theirs in town. They say it takes a village to raise a child, and Belle had a village. Between her husband's family and the neighbours, she wasn't alone. I envied my mom growing up with that village and loved visiting there. My attachment to the tiny hamlet remained long after those who were part of Mom's village died.

I think about Belle as I scrub carrots I harvested for soup. Some are no bigger than the tip of my finger. Once I would have tossed them in the bucket I keep for compost or thrown them in the trash. Now, I take time to scrub every single tiny one. I won't have enough for the soup—I'll supplement with a few from my crisper drawer—but I'm determined to use the ones I grew from seed and tended for months too. As a child, I heard stories about the Great Depression when Belle's family waited for the train to deliver potatoes—and how thankful they were to get the tubers that kept them from starving. Belle would have seen these tiny carrots as precious. I honour her struggle by using them.

One morning when I was twelve, my sister and I were getting ready for school when the phone rang. My grandmother had died overnight. Belle wasn't the type of grandma who said "I love you" or held babies on her lap.

She hadn't endeared herself to me and, years later, I wasn't surprised when I learned she chose not to add my sister's and my name to her family Bible (I assume because we were adopted). Days later when mom went through dresser drawers in Belle's bedroom, she found unopened packages of flannel nightgowns she had purchased for her mom over the years. Belle's nightgowns became mine. I wore the warm, floor-length granny gowns for years and found comfort in them. There were so many and they never seemed to wear out.

My grandmother had little influence over my life when she was alive but I've come to appreciate her strength and wish I could have known her better. It's the hamlet of Benson where she raised her little family that has lived in my memories and imagination more than anything. It comforts me, in this world of transient living and loose connection, to think about a community pulling together to support a young widow. I imagine heaven's a little like that prairie village.

Laura is often on my mind too. I imagine taking a break from my work to sit at the kitchen table, enjoy a cup of cinnamon tea, and chat about my now-grown children, Laurinda and Michael, with her. They were so little when she died. She would have loved watching them grow. Laura was nineteen in 1948 when she married Ed, a dashing soldier eleven years her elder who promised her three things: a house, a diamond ring, and a fur coat. A man of integrity, Dad delivered on all three. Laura always dreamed of being a mother, but her dreams died slowly when years passed and she didn't conceive. I imagine her quiet joy when they adopted me and, two years later, when they added another baby girl to our little family. Mom had no hobbies and few interests outside of her family. She was fifty-three when Dad died, and it seemed she lost both her purpose and her husband. She died suddenly eighteen months later. Her unmade choices, and a determination for something more in my life, largely influenced the woman I became.

Sometimes my thoughts turn to Mary and I wish she were among the ghosts who visit as I work but that's impossible. I've built up thick walls. It's safer that way. One day I'll appreciate her story and, though I'll never understand the root, I'll believe her choices came from a place of deep pain and will have empathy for her and the burdens she must have carried. But not quite yet.

Laurinda and Michael, come in my imaginings too. I wish I had parented them better. Like most parents, I look back and think of things I wish I had done differently. Sometimes guilt over choices I made influencing the home they grew up in weighs heavy. Consequences of choices Mary made all those years ago filtered down, influencing how I felt about myself and what I allowed in my life. It impacted the way I loved those I loved most. One day I'll find it in my heart to see Mary through eyes of compassion. One day I'll manage the same for myself.

My five-year-old red-haired granddaughter is the sweetest of all the ones who join me in my imagining.

Makiya is the shining star in my life. She is always in my heart, my prayers, and often on the screen of my tablet when we Skype as I work.

I run washed carrots under the tap one last time and lay them across the cutting board. Picking up the knife I hear Gerry's voice in the back of my mind. *Wouldn't it be easier if you used the Cuisinart?* Yes, it would be easier and faster but I wouldn't get the same satisfaction I do from the old-fashioned methodical *thunk thunk* of my knife on a wooden cutting board. I wouldn't feel the same tactile connection. Making soup—all of this garden and kitchen work—is meditation. It's busywork, yes, and it's crossed over the line to obsession, but in the chopping of vegetables and rumination of things in absentia, even though I don't realize it, I'm working things out and making way for a presence.

The timer goes off. The tomatoes have reached the end of their processing time and I lift the canner from the hot burner to the other side of the stove to let the pressure drop. I tip the cutting board of chopped carrots into the soup pot and move it to the still-warm burner. With my hands on my hips I stretch my back and imagine the satisfaction I'll feel on a cold, snowy winter day when I grab a pint of this soup from the shelf for lunch.

The phone rings. The number on the screen is one of the few I pick up for, so I rinse and dry my hands before answering.

"Hi, Grandma! Wanna Skype?"

Yes, sweet girl, I want to Skype. And with that, the ghosts disappear.

———————

There won't be many more warm days. Fall is already in the air. Summer came early, and with a vengeance. It's not surprising autumn is doing the same. Amidst rumours of frost I pick the remaining tomatoes from the vines. Now my windowsill is full of plump Brandywines; mysterious and soon-to-be-dark-and-delicious Black Krims; and long, slender Federle paste tomatoes. I'm tired and welcome the excuse to put the garden to rest. When I think about the volume of harvest and the busy days I spent canning the bounty, it's hard to believe I lay awake some nights in the early spring worrying my garden wouldn't produce. What's that they say? Ninety-nine percent of the things we worry about never come to pass. Now, the ground lies fallow where radishes, lettuce, carrots, and beets once grew. I'm still harvesting from the second planting of green beans, tall kale stalks that look like miniature palm trees, and rainbow Swiss chard a light frost won't bother. Soon the leaves will turn colour, I'll pack away capri pants, and pull out jeans and sweaters. I'm looking forward to the change of seasons bringing time with which I can curl up under a quilt with a book and a cup of tea—in effect, to not being so busy. That's the story I tell myself.

Chapter 4

DARK NIGHT

*One of the greatest of spiritual attainments
is the capacity to do nothing.*

Dallas Willard, *The Divine Conspiracy*

The sun drops lower on the horizon and the days grow shorter. My canning shelves are lined with jars filled with an assortment ranging from sweet red strawberry jam to thick, green split pea soup and the freezer is fat with fruit and fish. Like the ant in Aesop's *Ant and the Grasshopper* fable, who laboured instead of leisured during the long, hot days of summer, I rest as the cadence of summer gives way to a season in which there is time to ruminate on those untamed things that the busyness of tending a garden and preserving food keep at bay. I spend afternoons in my "woman cave" photographing dead and dying things plucked from the yard before the first hard frost. A friend offers a bouquet of dead birthday roses and I accept with gratitude, seeing beauty and melancholy in their crispy, wizened state. Quiet hours spent arranging things on a table next to the north-facing window and taking photos in the challenging autumn light replace the fervour of summer.

I try to write. I cough out a paragraph or two, but something always catches like an engine that has run out of oil and seized. I can't find the lubricant needed to get things moving again. Natalie Goldberg's words tacked to the wall above my desk mock me: "Write what disturbs you, what you fear, what you have not been willing to speak about. Be willing to be split open." Fear of fracturing keeps me from writing anything of substance.

Then a crack develops in an important relationship. The reason is less important than what happens as a result and I won't write a story that's not mine to share. The sliver of the other person's story that intersects mine is enough because at the core our stories of wonder and woe are remarkably similar. I trust you will understand the pain of a relational rift. The point is a chasm develops and it hurts. Wild things, hissing lies I'm unable to ignore, creep in. *Everyone leaves. No one wants you. You're not worthy.* They lie like a pride of lions with tails flicking truth like flies, yawning and exposing teeth as sharp as razors, watching me watch them. I'm bereft as my old foes of abandonment and rejection lift their ugly, long-toothed, soul-sucking heads and my world goes dark. I spiral down into an abyss and the darkness looks more inviting than anything else.

C.S. Lewis includes a note in the appendix of his classic work, *The Problem of Pain*, from R. Havard, M.D. based on his clinical experience: "Mental pain is less dramatic than physical pain but it is more common and also more hard to bear. The frequent attempt to conceal mental pain increases the burden."[3] I'm overwhelmed with the weight of emotion and the effort of holding it in. I isolate, huddled in a dark place, afraid of feelings that overwhelm. My body, tricky thing it is, manifests grief in physical pain. Havard says it's easier to tell someone we have a toothache than a broken heart, so perhaps there is some instinctual wisdom in this.

One morning, I'm standing in the shower with my hands on the wall letting the warm spray hit the part of my lower back that seems to be the angriest. The physical pain is a blessing. It's something tangible I can point to as the source of my discomfort. I'd like to stay in the shower but I'm weary and sluggish from another restless night and it would be too easy to close my eyes and fall asleep where I stand. I straighten, turn, and reach for the shampoo. The effort is like moving through Jell-O. This sluggish sense of pushing through tells me what I haven't wanted to admit: I'm depressed. *Hello, darkness, my old friend.*

Twenty-plus years earlier when my first marriage ended, I entered a season of darkness that, when I found the courage to poke at it, turned out to be about more than grief over a broken marriage. My divorce triggered a depression that thundered down on top of me like an avalanche as I grieved the loss of my heritage, my family of origin, Laura, Ed, Mary, and Belle's village where she and, for a short time, I belonged to a place and a people.

I spent long and sleepless nights thinking about what it would be like to fall apart, wondering how a person surrendered. I wanted to give up but I didn't know how. Letting go seemed a luxury I couldn't afford as a now-single parent. I put one foot in front of the other, went to the office every day and did the job they paid me well to do. I parented—not as well as I wish, but the best way I could given the state I was in. I sat in my therapist's office broken and crying week after week until I was certain my heart would explode. Finally, empty and with nowhere else to turn, I let go. I pulled back, got quiet, and listened. In time, healing came as I dwelled in solitude and silence. I wrestled with depression for years, digging at the root so I could eradicate a little more each time. I made gradual progress and thought by now I was finished.

We don't like to think of ourselves as self-absorbed, but we are. What we see, touch, taste, hear, and smell shapes our reality. Our senses, the ebbing and flowing of our emotions, and our sometimes-muddled thoughts influence how we experience the world. Most of us mature and grow past the baby stage of thinking everything revolves around us. We come to understand we're one of many and the ripples of our life intersect with others around us. Somewhere along the way we realize our sensory experience is only part of reality and there's an unseen dimension. We wrestle as we try to understand it—don't believe anyone who tells you they don't. It's okay. It's in the wrestling where we find our faith.

But in depression we're at the centre again. Overwhelmed with pain bigger and louder than anything else, we feel alone and lose sight of the community we feel unworthy of belonging to. We lose hope and find ourselves at a precipice. There's a chasm in front of us so deep we can't see the bottom. We sense oppressive, dank darkness as we lean out and peer into the abyss. We face a choice: stay where we are, physically safe but in debilitating emotional pain, or attempt to jump the chasm to see what's on the other side. We see green grass and lush vegetation over there. The risk of jumping could be one worth taking.

A third option—one we hesitate to entertain—forms in our minds in the darkest times: step off and free fall into the abyss. The nothingness is mesmerizing and strangely inviting. The absence of the pain would be a relief. A siren song rises from the dark and we stretch out trying to see what's down there. Many of us know something of that enticement. The only thing certain is we can't turn back. So, what to do? Stay or move forward? Hold on or let go? Which choice is the right one? How do we take the first step?

I step out of the shower and wrap a towel around my aching body knowing something I didn't when I got in: I'm depressed. As I lean in toward the mirror and peer into the empty eyes looking back at me, I tell myself I came through it before and can do so again. I try to recall what brought me out of the darkness last time and remember there is another way—one I have been too absorbed in my pain to see—grace.

———————

The word that comes to my mind as weeks pass and I wrestle in the darkness is *deep*. Deep pain. Deep despair. Deep disappointment. Deep discouragement. Surely, somewhere amidst all this there must be a measure of deep healing, joy, and hope too. I feel the need to pray but struggle to believe my prayers matter. Do I have the faith to ask for divine will to supersede my own? Do I believe in such a thing as God's best? And, if so, how painful will surrendering to that *best* turn out to be? I am the duck, still paddling with a peaceful smile on my duck face but plagued by a darkness so thick my body aches from the effort of pushing through it.

One Sunday morning, I'm standing next to Gerry in church during worship time and find I'm unable to open my mouth. I look around at others standing with hands and voices lifted in praise and wonder how it can be no one senses what's happening to me in the back row. I'm utterly shattered. The effort of holding myself somewhat together is more than I can manage. I'm raw and bleeding and it takes every bit of strength I can muster to hold myself in check. Then it's too much and I sit down, feeling worse for having done so. I can't even find it within myself to offer praise. Add "ungrateful" to the list of charges against me.

I sit with my eyes straight ahead as Gerry rests a hand on my shoulder and the worship team moves into another song. I bow my head. *Help!* is the only prayer I can muster. I wish for a kind word or a comforting hug beyond my husband's hand resting on my shoulder, but I hope for neither. The slightest kindness will start an outpouring, and I'm certain that to let the tiniest bit out will release a torrent of grief so monumental it might never stop. I should have stayed at home. There's nothing I can offer or receive here. Stoicism is my saviour this morning.

I sit through the rest of the service, numb. When we're dismissed, Gerry leaves to tend to something in the church office and I remain sitting in the sanctuary. I strike a bargain with God: *if you're there, send someone.* But God doesn't barter in bargains and there's nothing in my countenance to invite anyone to come and sit with me. People mill around in groups, drinking coffee and laughing, while I sit arrow-straight with my eyes focused on nothing at the front of the sanctuary. The poet, Henry Wadsworth Longfellow knew "oftentimes we call a man cold when he is only sad."[4] I wish for a someone with a poet's heart to see it's only my "secret sorrow which the world knows not"[5] keeping me in this solitary space, but there are no poets in church this morning.

———————

Later, I toss a handful of bath salts in the tub, gather some supplies—a glass of ice water, a candle, my phone, and earbuds—and seek escape in the comfort of a hot bath. I call up a playlist on my phone I call *Comfort*, settle back in the warm water, and close my eyes. Some might call it self-pity, but in such a state I'm in it's the only all-encompassing thing. *Why is this happening again? Why does everyone leave? What's wrong with me?* I listen to the music as movies from my past replay in my mind. Grief falls from my eyes as I rip off scabs leaving me wounded and bloody. The past taught me the only way out of grief is through it. I know I need to dive in and start swimming but I've forgotten how.

I realize a song is repeating, so I pick up my phone and switch the playlist to shuffle. Another song plays, then the same one again. This time I pay attention to the words. The singer sings of a constant divine presence shining through when he needs it most and I remember God carried me through depression before. Through endless, sleepless, prayer-filled nights. Through hours of scribbling in my notebook. And, in relief coming, not in a moment, but over a season. The words of the song remind me of that faithfulness. I wonder if a playlist be an answer to prayer. I believe it can, and I believe it is.

———————

On another restless night I try to resist the storm that keeps me from resting. I thrash around: too warm and then too cool. I struggle to find a position comfortable enough to allow the nothingness of sleep to come. My body aches. I try to pray.

Help. Where are you? Are you there?

My prayers seem to hit the ceiling and fall to the floor beside my bed. I reach for my eReader and open a book I turn to in the night when I have trouble sleeping. Years ago, when I struggled with sleeplessness, my doctor suggested I stop tossing and turning, get out of bed, and read a book reserved only for such times. I never followed his advice. Those were working years, and I was too busy fretting about how few hours were left until I had to get up and how tired I was going to be at work. It's different now.

He's been dead for more than five hundred years but through ancient language falling like pearls, Thomas à Kempis in *The Imitation of Christ* reminds me of truth as fresh as the day he wrote it.

"Strive, therefore, to turn away thy heart from the love of the things that are seen, and to set it upon the things that are not seen."[6] Take your eyes off of what you think you see and set them on the truth you know, Linda. God has not left you.

"Foolish out of measure is he who attendeth upon other things rather than those which serve to his soul's health."[7] I've spent so much effort on keeping busy to keep from hurting. The constant doing kept the unmanageable, painful things under control, but it has done nothing to benefit the health of my soul.

"We must not trust every word of others or feeling within ourselves, but cautiously and patiently try the matter, whether it be of God."[8] Those accusing whispers I hear? Not trustworthy. Not worthy of my attention.

"Seek a suitable time for thy meditation," Kempis says. "Think frequently of the mercies of God to thee."[9] And in the middle of the night while my husband and Yorkie slumber beside me, I take inventory of simple ordinary gifts: the harvest moon, orange and yellow fall mums in bloom, sweet Sungold tomatoes. Grace.

And finally: "Ask freely, and hear in silence."[10] Ask, be still, and listen. Trust that when I listen, answers will come.

———————————

Before one can climb out of the abyss, there must be a point at which you hit bottom. It can be a hard fall that shatters you, or a gentle landing on the bottom and a sense you're not going any deeper. Every day I pray: *please let this day be my lowest*. I mix up a synergy with essential oils and hold the inhaler to my nose throughout the day. I take hot bath after hot bath and the gentle music coming through my earbuds washes me as much as the scented bathwater. An honest conversation with someone who has also walked through depression and understands the physical manifestations helps me remember I'm not the only one who has navigated a dark night such as this and made my way through.

"If you look for truth, you may find comfort in the end"[11] says C.S. Lewis. "If you look for comfort you will not get either comfort or truth—only soft soap and wishful thinking to begin with and, in the end, despair."[12] I need a little soft-soap soul care but it doesn't penetrate deep enough to touch the root of what has taken me down. For that I need truth.

So, I close the French doors to our den, answer neither phone call nor text message, and feel no guilt at sequestering myself away. In solitude and silence, I read scripture aloud and write through the hard things that have knocked me off balance. I stop looking for answers to questions I can't articulate and simply sit in God's presence. And there, in the transforming furnace of solitude that Henri Nouwen calls the "place of the great struggle, and the great encounter,"[13] I wrestle my false self and the divine whisper I couldn't hear when I was running (or paddling my webbed feet to the point of exhaustion) breaks through. I stumble into the arms of "the loving God who offers himself as the substance of the new self."[14] I see the depth of my brokenness has no correlation to my worth. I'm a created being loved without condition. Who I am isn't the result of anything I do or altered by anything done to me. Who I am is beloved. What if I stopped trying to be anything else?

For years, I put great stock in independence and ability. Whether it was debugging a computer program or executing a project plan, tending a productive garden or keeping a well-stocked larder, I earned a seat at the table through what I accomplished. I began to see the folly of this before I retired. I knew I was staking my worth on a lie. I thought in retirement I'd find a better way but the only thing that changed was what busy looked like. I've done none of the things I planned to do: taken a solitary walk in the park, sat in a coffee shop to write, or spent an entire day with a book. I've written nothing of note. Writing is a mosaic of thought and intuition, wisdom and wonder, and I've allowed myself an opportunity for none of those things.

Work and being busy aren't inherently bad. I'm glad my health care provider is busy seeing patients and keeping up to date on current research and treatment, but I hope she balances it with periods of sitting in silence to listen. That's where wisdom, not knowledge, increases. I'm glad those who govern our country, keep our economy moving, grow our food, and manufacture the things we need, are making a living. I pray they're also taking time to craft a life. When busyness becomes the thing through which we derive our self-worth, or the diversion we use to keep from feeling, it shifts from being necessary and important to self-destructive and soul-sucking.

Busy isn't the balm we need to heal. Busy work isn't work at all, it's just a place to hide from the wild things. The real work comes in stillness when we're brave enough to face the things that startle us in the night, to stand at the opening to a cave of unknowing and take the first step forward. The propensity toward using busyness as a salve is the same one driving addicts to use substances that crush their souls. It's the same thing that drew Mary to look for comfort in the arms of men undeserving of her, leaving her with the permanent pain of a mother separated from her children. It's the same thing that kept me running and prevented me from facing my adversaries of abandonment and rejection.

"Joy does not simply happen to us,"[15] says Henri Nouwen. "We have to choose joy and keep choosing it every day."[16] So, I choose. I pay attention to whispers and wonder and write about ordinary God-glorifying moments in daily blog posts. They are as much for me as they are for those who come to my virtual home to read them. They keep me on track. Sometimes where I start isn't where I end up. I stumble on something with which I need to go deeper, and I move to my private journal where I work things out by tapping out words that turn into prayer. I hear a sweet whisper and isn't that sometimes the purpose of prayer after all? Less a presenting of requests and more a surrender of self as we labour and listen and become transformed into the image bearers we are.

Daily, sometimes hourly, I remind myself of truth I am learning in my great encounter—I am loved without condition. I ride a gradual return to strength but the grief never completely leaves. It's always there, just below the surface, ready to stomp in like an indignant child at the slightest opportunity. An anonymous 14th century sojourner wrote of a time in which "you'll only experience a darkness, like a cloud of unknowing"[17] and it is like that for a time. I know there's something—some *One*—but I still see so dimly. *I believe. Help my unbelief.* "Make your home in the darkness. Stay there as long as you can,"[18] he says. "It's the closest you can get to God here on earth, by waiting in this darkness and in this cloud."[19] So, day by day, I make my way through the darkness.

It seems obvious, like those hidden pictures-with-in-pictures of dots and colours that you have to really focus on to see, but once you've seen it you see it easily and always. Seeking significance through glowing performance evaluations or stocked canning shelves is folly. I'll never find self-worth in deadlines met, projects completed, or mason jars filled. Mind-numbing busyness is a liar only magnifying sneers of abandonment and rejection that still somehow weave their way into my mind.

That same 14th century seeker wrote of lifting one's "heart up to God with a gentle stirring of love; wanting him, and not anything he's made."[20] As Augustine said: "our heart is restless until it rests in thee."[21] There's no tangible or intangible thing, no matter how lovely, that will satisfy my longing. It's the heart of my Creator I've hungered after all these years.

We're taking a road trip, north to see our kids. The sky is blue, the sun is shining, and the snow in the fields beside the road is a brilliant white. I've seen nothing like it before. It's magic. The snow-adorned weeds and brush alongside the road catch the sun and sparkle as if sprinkled with fairy dust. I watch the twinkling, brilliant and beautiful, as we pass mile after mile. I wish I could capture in a photograph what I'm seeing with my eyes, but no camera lens could do it justice.

It's December, and glittery Christmas garland is everywhere. It's gaudy compared to this natural wonder. Likewise, all my desires and hopes, my grief and my sorrow pales in comparison to the divine presence I met in the great encounter.

A few miles down the road we drive through a fog bank and the sparkle of the sun-kissed snow disappears. Visibility is difficult and Gerry reduces his speed to safely navigate the curves. I know well that sense of being in the gray. Before long we're out of the fog, driving past snowy fields bathed in the sunshine again. The magic sparkle of a few miles back is no more because we've changed direction and the sun is higher in the sky. My human eye no longer sees the glitter but my spiritual eye knows it's still there. It just takes the right light to make it visible again. I think about how the light can restore the joy in my heart too. Never mind the fog or a change of direction, divine light can penetrate it all. I can choose to look at my circumstances through natural eyes or with supernatural vision. More and more, I'm choosing supernatural.

———————

Winter gives way to the promise of another spring. One afternoon I'm driving down Main street on the way to my community garden plot to toss radish seeds in the ground. I'm thinking about the things I learned in my great encounter and, while I'm grateful, I'm not satisfied. I want to go deeper so I pray a simple prayer: *God, please let me feel your love.*

I have no way of knowing I'm on the cusp of an even greater encounter than the one that took place in the solitude and silence of my den. It will forever change me.

Chapter 5
FEAR AND FAITH

The important thing is to recognize that our gift, no matter what the size, is indeed something given us, for which we can take no credit, but which we may humbly serve, and, in serving, learn more wholeness, be offered wondrous newness.

Madeleine L'Engle,
Walking on Water: Reflections on Faith and Art

It's not yet dawn, and I'm sitting upright in our king-sized bed tapping out words on my tablet for a daily blog post. In these first hours of the day I watch the sun rise over the hills through the east-facing door leading from our bedroom to the deck and read, write, pray, and dance with words.

"What time is it?" Gerry mumbles as he rises toward wakefulness.

"It's too early for you," I whisper. "Go back to sleep."

He tugs on the duvet, rolls over, and soon his steady breathing rhythm confirms he's fallen asleep.

I open the WordPress editor and type in today's date. Every morning, a habit guiding my first thoughts of the day: one of my photos and a few words about thin places where the divine intersects the ordinary. I come to the virtual page with intention: to declare the supernatural glory, remind myself of wisdom gleaned in my great encounter, and contribute kindness to the collective conversation.

The world feels noisy and unsafe. Like Robert Benson, "the speed and pace of our life here in this country, the noise and the demand of it, the sheer unadulterated motion of it, are almost too much for me to cope with."[22] I am overwhelmed. But it's more than the breakneck pace with which we're encouraged, and expected, to race through our days wearing me down. The daily news cycle and social media cacophony fuels a propensity to lash out at those with beliefs or opinions contrary to our own and makes me want to withdraw and move to a mountaintop. We no longer trust one another. We're tempted to close our ears and our sensibilities to anyone who perceives things in a different light. We've become tribal rather than communal, viewing those we call *other* with disdain, despite our claims of inclusivity. I write to counteract the anxiety I feel and serve up something kinder.

———————

I buy a new Moleskine notebook—any excuse to pick up another notebook—with which to scribble thoughts in a manner more tactile than tapping them out on a keyboard. Maybe the physicality of writing that way might get those synapses firing again. I decide I need a new desk to go with the new notebook and I position it facing out from the picture window in my office toward the ridge.

I declare the desk an electronic-free zone and cover the USB station in the corner with a pen and pencil receptacle. My other desk, the one I bought when I was writing *Two Hearts* sits across the room in front of my bookshelf. There, my laptop, a second monitor, papers, notebooks, and other assorted oddities clutter the top. It's my get-stuff-done desk. When I bring my phone or another device into the room, I put it on the get-stuff-done desk to preserve the quiet, unplugged, and contemplative mood of the new writing desk. I arrange a few things on top: the Moleskine, a cup with coloured highlighters, a few of my favourite gel pens, a coaster for my ever-present glass of ice water, and a bottle of rosemary essential oil to stimulate my brain.

One afternoon I come home to find a large bouquet of cut flowers on the corner of my writing desk—red roses, white spider mums, and other flowers I don't know the name of. A gift. A christening of my space. I thank Gerry for his thoughtfulness and ask him not to touch my desk again. I'm only half joking.

I fill the right-hand drawer with Post-it notes, index cards, and coloured pencils. The large drawer on the left becomes home to the shitty first draft[23] of a book manuscript, the clipped together outline, character sketches, and start of a novel I brought with me from Washington. I set a goal to write three pages of *something* in the Moleskine every day.

I dabble with characters and scenes, write a few short stories, and pull out the bones of the novel. I sit at my new desk and look out the window at the ridge across the valley. I stand, pace back and forth, and open my Bible for inspiration. I move to my get-stuff-done desk and Google fairy and folk tales, looking for one to capture my fancy and springboard into a story. My brain hurts from the effort of it all. Do I have the skill to write fiction? To craft characters, a world, and a story from nothing? More important: do I have the desire? Writing fiction seems safer than slicing open my chest and trying to write another memoir. I can hide many things under cover of "it's just a story." But is it the kind of writing I want to do?

I ruminate about this in the Moleskine one afternoon (mostly so I can get three pages filled for the day) and uncover a reason for my creative block: a belief in my inadequacy. See the subtlety? It's not a belief my writing is inadequate keeping me from committing to a long-form project, it's that I'm inadequate. I see the self-centeredness in choosing to hold on to these thoughts and how it gives more credence to my insecurities than the power of love.

What if I embrace the inherent characteristics I see as short-comings as gifts? What if I fess up to the fact my hobbies are reading and writing and that I never really liked hiking? Can my quiet-loving, often-awkward, and introspective nature be used to accomplish my God-given purpose? Isn't that the way it's supposed to be?

The world tells me I'm not enough. I'm not outgoing or talented enough, and my paltry offerings of words are not good enough. The world tells me to don a mask of accomplishment and competency and invites me to compare my life with the filtered and curated reality of others. It tells me I have to be more, do more, and if I'm to be a writer, promote, promote, promote. But love tells me something different.

Love tells me I am created with purpose and I fulfill it by using the resources I'm given to walk, not hike, through ordinary days. Rather than trying to conform to an imaginary standard against which I'll always come up short, what if I use who I am *as I am* to draw the attention of others toward the holy grace of this life? Find fresh ways to write timeless truth for the benefit of others: that seems a worthy goal.

A composer works out his longing in the notes of a symphony. A poet strings words together like pearls to paint word pictures. An artist sees light and reflection and nuances of colour and shapes, inspiring her to create something tangible to reflect that which cannot be contained.

Those called to create do so to the glory of God whether we realize it or not.

Writing about my faith terrifies me. But God's only begotten didn't sweat blood and endure atrocities I can't fathom so I can sit in the comfort of my bed in the early morning, sipping soy milky frothy coffee, saying it wasn't enough. How selfish to take the abilities given me, look into the eyes of the giver, mumble "thanks," then toss them into the bushes. *Thank you but it's not enough to give me the confidence I need to do the work of serving others. I'll sit here on the sidelines and let someone with more confidence, a stronger gift, and a better way of wrangling words find fresh ways to write timeless truth. My meagre portion isn't enough. If you wanted me to do more, you should have given me more.*

Ouch.

———————

Gerry and I pack our cameras and take a late-afternoon drive to a place neither of us has been before. He drives a winding bumpy road and we look for things of interest to stop and photograph. The ruts in front of us get deeper as we climb higher on a road leading somewhere-but-we're-not-sure-where. I'm filled with fear.

We arrive at the top of the mountain, get out of the car, and look out over the valley below. The view is breathtaking. We're surrounded by pure and sweet silence. I'm not enjoying it because I'm afraid.

We get back in the car and Gerry drives a short way farther. He stops, gets out of the car, and walks over to get a closer look at a rickety structure that's barely hanging on to the ridge. I wait in the car watching whispers of clouds brush by as he walks to the edge. I imagine a storyline and think I might pull out my notebook to jot down a few words. I realize the story I'm imagining is rooted in fear.

I wonder about this fear, my faith, and the desire to write. I think about intentions, fits and starts, and the half-written things tucked away in my desk drawer, on the hard drive of my laptop, and in the cloud. Writing fiction seems safer, but life-writing—conquering fear and risking vulnerability by sharing a slice of my life to illustrate a universal truth—that's the writing I want to do.

I think about the tabernacle, the torn curtain, the blood-bought confidence I'm afraid to walk in, and how intention hasn't done what I expected it to. I hunger for something more creatively substantial than daily blog meditations within which to express the grace in which I'm clothed. When Madeleine L'Engle found herself in a creativity slump, she played the piano. Einstein found playing the violin broke the barrier between his conscious and unconscious mind, allowing intuition to manifest in the wonder of creativity. Gardening could do it for me if I used it as a creative outlet rather than something to keep mindlessly busy with. I catch glimpses of the divine in the garden but I'm too focused on the work to pay attention to the wonder. I've missed the point entirely.

———————

I pray, listen, and poke the pile of fear to see what's there. I'm certain, on a day when I am stronger, I'll toss the smelly, oily canvas aside and reveal nothing—no power, not one thing with the power to take me down—that it's all a pile of lies. Some days I struggle to maintain my faith amidst day-to-day circumstances. Sometimes I wallow in self-pity and sometimes I stay in there for a while. The pain feels like it's more than I can cope with some days. Wearing a mask of having it all together chafes.

But God understands our seasons of doubt and doesn't love us any less for them. The Creator invites us to draw near in those dark times; they're opportunities to go deeper. Wearing the prettiest I've-got-it-all-together mask was never the point—love was always the point. Dropping our guard is okay even when it's hard.

Then, one morning love whispers and God uses an emotion-packed word to speak clearer to me than ever before. I'm touched in the deep place where unworthiness festers, and I am changed.

PART 2
Broken

Chapter 6
CHOSEN

But I beg you, do not surrender the word "chosen" to the world. Dare
to claim it as your own, even when it is constantly misunderstood.
You must hold on to the truth that you are the chosen one. That
truth is the bedrock on which you can build a life as the Beloved.

Henri J.M. Nouwen, *Life of the Beloved*

A symphony of birdsong and sweet-scented morning air
fills the room. It's already hot. We haven't switched on the
air conditioning, preferring instead open windows and
doors to allow finch songs and fresh air to pour into the
house after the long, dark closed-in days of winter. I lay still
in this liminal zone, as Gerry dozes next to me and Maya
snores at the foot of the bed, thinking about the day ahead.

I want to go to my community garden plot to sow radish, lettuce, and turnip seeds. Should I pull out the spinach already bolting in the early heat of the season? It will mean an end to daily spinach salads, but I can't wait much longer because I have cucumber and summer squash plants waiting to be planted in the space. I need to stop at the store and pick up a few things, make a batch of yogurt, and I want to send photos to the lab. If I tend to those things early, maybe I'll be able to spend time on the deck with a book this afternoon. With varying degrees of success, I'm trying harder to maintain a balance between doing and being.

I reach for my tablet and pop into my cloud folder. Soon, there will be flowers in the garden to photograph but not yet. I select a photo I took of a pink grocery store osteospermum a few days ago for my daily blog post and browse through a folder of saved quotations looking for one to pair with the image. "It is a time of quiet joy, the sunny morning. When the glittery dew is on the mallow weeds, each leaf holds a jewel which is beautiful if not valuable. This is no time for hurry or bustle. Thoughts are slow and deep and golden in the morning."[24] Thank you, John Steinbeck. The words reflect the peace with which I ease into the day and pair well with the photo. I open another browser window, create a new blog post, add the quote and the photo, tap out a morning meditation, and click publish. Then, I reach for my Bible.

My reading takes me to a place I've read from many times in a translation unfamiliar to me. It's a letter written by a man named Peter to people living in what is now Turkey. It starts with the standard greetings and salutations—who it's from and who it's written to—like the *Dear Linda* part of a modern-day letter. I usually skim over these introductory phrases, but this morning something stops me. It's as if I'm reading the words for the first time and they are addressed directly to me: *God . . . knew you and chose you long ago.*[25] I know the words were written on papyrus to first-century Jewish Christians but somehow this morning they're whispered, deep unto deep, only to me.

My senses are heightened in a way I never imagined possible. I can't read any further. The word and the concept I eschewed all my life—*chosen*—is suddenly inexplicably and unmistakeably mine. But it's not the chosen-from-a-room-full-of-babies word whispering abandonment that washes over me. It's not exclusive, inclusive, or anything but pure and personal love.

I sit with a truth so clear there's no doubting it. I'm still sitting with it when Gerry gets up to make coffee and I'm still sitting with it when he returns with two frothy mugs, puts one on the bedside table next to me, reaches for my hand and says good morning, then pads over to the other side of the bed to retrieve his tablet. In silence I take the first sip of coffee.

I'm here, but somehow also elsewhere, floating on love. I can't explain it. It wouldn't make sense if I tried. I don't know why, or how, or anything other than pure ineffable love. I see the consolation prize role I played for almost sixty years is a lie. My struggles with feeling rejected and unworthy are not the most powerful thing in the narrative of my life. My physical issues, social awkwardness, fears, and anxieties don't disqualify me from anything. The rough invisibility cloak I slipped into early and have worn for most of my life despite how it chafes, is no more. A mantilla of being known replaces it. It's as if I've tossed aside the smelly, oily canvas that I was afraid covered something terrifying and, just as I suspected, found nothing underneath.

For days I return to the same place in scripture every morning. I can't move past it. I ruminate on the words and speak them aloud to myself throughout the day. I write them on an index card and carry it around with me. Colours seem more vivid, the scent of spring, sweeter. Love, something tangible.

It will be months before I remember my prayer that afternoon when I was driving to the community garden: *God, please let me feel your love.* In time, I will come to believe this early morning encounter is an answer to that prayer but for now, I can't see the experience through any lens other than awe.

————————

I grew up under the shadow of having been chosen, told often the story of being picked from a room full of babies to be Ed and Laura's daughter. Following advice given by well-meaning professionals, they intended the story to implant a sense of significance and belonging in the heart of a child who lost all connection with her heritage. It was meant to assist with the business of grafting me into my new family. But what I heard in the story was *consolation prize* because, surely, Ed and Laura would have preferred to conceive a child of their own.

To be chosen also meant rejected. That I was available to be chosen meant the woman who should have loved me more than anyone else did not keep me. Chosen was a burden. It meant abandoned and rejected. I never wanted to be chosen.

I turn to my thesaurus to see if there's another word I can use in its place when I think about the scripture because *chosen* still chafes. The antonyms—ignored and inferior—are the descriptors I've felt most at home with. In what the thesaurus describes as the concepts of the word *chosen,* I find something more meaningful: indebted and radical, worthwhile and worthy, dependent and unique. Yes. That's what I heard in the divine whisper.

I say silent prayers before I write a word: *What should I say?* And the answer is always the same: *love.* I've heard some say we focus too much on love and not enough on truth and I say they haven't experienced what I did that morning when love was the only thing. My perspective changes as I look for the divine in the everyday. My writing changes as I become brave. My photography changes as I seek to capture something glory-giving in my images. My response to everything is prayer, and the answer is always the same: *love*. I see the thing that will satisfy me is the very thing I was created for: connection to my Creator.

Chapter 7

ONCE YOU ARE REAL

"Real isn't how you are made," said the Skin Horse. "It's a thing that happens to you . . . once you are Real you can't be ugly, except to people who don't understand."

Margery Williams Bianco, *The Velveteen Rabbit*

Mary was four months pregnant in August 1958 when she sat across a desk at the social services offices in Regina, Saskatchewan. Merlin was alert and active, as any four-year-old child would be, but the caseworker noted he seemed to act out Mary's insecurity and she over-indulged him. She thought her son would "get beyond [Mary] and she [would] not be able to handle him alone."[26] Certainly Mary was incapable of caring for a second child—her lack of financial resources notwithstanding. That's the narrative the worker jotted down as she looked over her glasses at the quiet, slightly cross-eyed, young woman on the other side of her desk. Instead of offering support to someone facing a difficult crossroads she had only judgment and suggested a single path of action.

Mary was not far enough along in her pregnancy to have felt her baby move and she "spoke very little of the coming child." She "seemed more concerned with her four-year-old boy." Part of her still hadn't accepted she was carrying another child—a child she felt she had no choice but to relinquish. Denial seemed the safer place to dwell. She believed the line she was fed, that it was "impossible for her to care for two children on her own resources." She told no one in her family about the pregnancy and expected no help. "She seems to feel more sorry for herself than she does for the child," noted the caseworker.

I was conflicted when I first read these things in my adoption file, still processing my feelings toward Mary. That she seemed to have had more concern for herself and Merlin justified my anger but now I have more empathy toward her than anything else. Society was not kind to pregnant unmarried women. Given opportunity and support, Mary might have kept me. As it was, the caseworker's impression of her sub-par parenting skills only reinforced her shame and sense of unworthiness, cementing the narrative that played over and over in her mind reminding her she had messed up once again. The so-called professionals played to her weakness, convincing her of her unworthiness instead of offering encouragement and options.

Mary compartmentalized what was happening so she could walk through it. I can't imagine how she could have done otherwise. She had to carry on for the sake of Merlin, but she must have wept when she was alone at night. The caseworker saw a woman with self-protective stoicism and little regard for her unborn baby. In reality, stuffing down her grief was the only way she could survive.

————————

Gerry sets three pieces of mail down on the kitchen counter.

"The one on the bottom is the important one."

I turn from slicing cucumbers, wipe my hands on a kitchen towel, and shuffle through the envelopes. I stop at the third one. It's from Saskatchewan Social Services.

Five months ago, when the province of Saskatchewan opened birth records to adoptees, I—like countless others adopted in the province—sent in the forms requesting my original birth registration. I expect no surprises on the form but I'm reluctant to open the envelope. I put it on the counter along with the rest of the mail and return to the cucumbers.

From there, I fold and put away laundry, water the flowers outside, wash the floors, and busy myself with a myriad of things for hours. Anything to avoid opening the envelope on the counter. Finally, late in the afternoon I can find no more distractions. I grab my tablet and the letter and head out to the deck.

There are two sheets of paper in the envelope. I skim over the cover letter and set it aside. The *Certificate of Live Birth* is what I've waited almost sixty years to see.

There, my place of birth (Regina, Saskatchewan), the name Mary gave me (Linda Louise Gunther), my weight (8 lb. 14 ½ oz.), and the length of her pregnancy (40 weeks). And a question: Are the parents married to each other? (No). Red x's next to my name cross-reference a notation, also in red, near the bottom of the document dated six months after my birth date. Name by adoption (Linda Gail Brauer), father by adoption (Edward Louis Brauer), and mother by adoption (Laura Donalda Brauer).

Below, there is a stroke through the section for the father's information and it stings. By now I know Mary was forthcoming with information about Frank; it's all there in the adoption file. But Mary and Frank weren't married to each other, so he was never legally my father, despite the fact that I shared his DNA. If Frank's name was on this form, it would be the single piece of paper tying my whole origin story together. I'm sorry it's not.

Mary's name and address are in the mother's information section, along with her citizenship (Canadian), racial origin (Dutch), age at the time of this birth (39 years), and occupation (housekeeper). The form shows she has had three pregnancies, including this one, and given birth to three children.

My eyes drop to her signature, dated the day after I was born. Her handwriting seems shaky. I wonder what it must have been like for her to sign this form. "Mother is quite disturbed in separation from child" a caseworker wrote on the intake slip putting me in the care of the Department of Social Welfare and Rehabilitation. The notation goes on to say her upset is magnified because she had given birth to a daughter. She is bereft. I can only imagine her grief.

It's such a sad document. I hold it for a while, then pick up my tablet and search for the address where Mary lived in Regina. I find a photograph of a tiny house that's obviously been updated over the years. It looks old enough. It could be the same one. It's a ten-minute walk from the Regina General Hospital where I was born. Did Mary rent it in the latter part of her pregnancy given its proximity to the hospital? Was it a home made available by the Saskatchewan Social Services or a religious organization, for pregnant and unmarried mothers intending on surrendering their babies to adoption?

I imagine Mary and four-year-old, Merlin, living there throughout the fall, Christmas, and in the dark of a harsh Saskatchewan January, waiting for labour to begin. What was going through her mind? Was she having second thoughts? Did she wish there was another way? Did she talk to her unborn baby and reassure her the choice she was making was for the best? What stories did she tell Merlin about the changes occurring in her body? It's a grace that I finally hold my top-secret birth registration in my hands and virtually return to the little house where Mary lived and waited, wrapped in divine love she probably didn't feel while she carried me.

After a while, I go into the house and hand the document to Gerry.

"How do you feel about this?" he asks.

"I'm uncomfortable," I admit. "I'm not sure why."

I'm trying to hold myself together and observe the surfacing emotions without getting caught up in them, like Mary must have done over and over in the months before I was born. Gerry questions something, sending me downstairs to retrieve the binder where I keep my adoption-related documentation. I leaf through the pages of my adoption file, a thick packet of information with black marks throughout to protect the identities of my birth and adoptive parents, all long dead by now, and pause at the court transcript of the day when Mary went before a judge.

There are five people present in the room: the judge, Mary, a stenographer, and a caseworker holding a two-month-old baby girl.[27] It's Mary's second appearance before this judge—the first with me present. The case was adjourned a month earlier to give caseworkers more time to locate Mary's husband, John. Having been unsuccessful, the caseworker brings Mary in to testify to her relationship with John hoping the judge will dispense with the formality.

It's been almost a decade since Mary had any contact with him. What is the point?

"Do you recognize the baby in court?" the judge asks after preliminary questions about Mary's family, her marital status, and religion.

Her eyes rest on the tiny face of the baby she has never held.

"Yes."

"Who is the mother of this child?"

"I am," Mary whispers.

For the record, he asks the baby's name, gender, birth-date, and place of birth.

And, inexplicably: "Has the baby been baptized?"

Mary has had no contact with her daughter since she was born. "Not that I know of."

"What would you like to have done with her? Can you keep her yourself?"

"I would like to but I can't."

"Is your husband the father of this child?" The judge knows all this; he's read the case notes. He asks for the benefit of the transcript, and to the detriment of Mary. Shame must have weighed heavy on her as she answered.

"No."

"Are you prepared to tell the court who is the father of this baby?"

She was, and she did.

"You have stated, Mary, that you feel you cannot look after the baby, Linda Louise Gunther. Could you tell the court why you feel this way?"

"Because I'd rather she had two parents instead of one."

Months of conversations with caseworkers convinced her the baby would be better off in the care of two married parents. They could give her stability, financial and otherwise, in ways Mary had no prospect of doing.

"Do you realize that if your child is committed as a ward of the Minister of Social Welfare and Rehabilitation that you lose all legal rights to the child?"

"Yes, I do."

"And that you cannot get her back?"

"Yes."

"Have you had enough time to think about it?"

"I think so."

She hadn't. There would never be enough time to convince her to believe there was anything right about relinquishing her daughter.

"Under the circumstances are you willing or unwilling to look after the baby?"

"It's not what I want. It's what's best for her."

This was the same sentiment Laura and Ed used when they tried to explain it to me. "She knew two parents were better than one. She wanted what was best for you." It's what unmarried mothers were told back then: you can't do it and we won't help you try.

The judge is firm in his belief that Mary's legal spouse, John, needs to be notified and he adjourns the case for another month. Mary is brought before the judge twice more before, finally, John is located and signs an affidavit. With sworn statements from both Mary and John divesting themselves of "custody and all legal rights" to me, and no sign of Frank, my biological father, the judge rules I am "a neglected child" and commits me to the care and custody of the ministry.

———————————

I wipe away tears and wonder what good can come of tearing these scabs off again. I pray the healing will go deeper this time because this birth registration makes it official: I was born and not dropped here out of nowhere. Real, like the Skin Horse in *The Velveteen Rabbit*. "It doesn't happen all at once . . . you become. It takes a long time. That's why it doesn't happen to people who break easily or have sharp edges."[28] As the Skin Horse told the Rabbit "generally, by the time you are Real, most of your hair has been loved off, and your eyes drop out and you get loose in the joints and very shabby."[29] I feel that worn out shabbiness but, after almost sixty years, it's happening to me. Holding this paper in my hand makes it true in my heart what was true all along: I'm capital-R Real. This proves it. I am raw and battle-weary but that's what it's like to be real.

Later, I put the binder and genealogy books away but leave the Certificate of Live Birth on the dining room table to remind me I'm real. Two days later, a friend gives me a celebratory bouquet of pink flowers—the kind you give someone when a baby girl is born. The gift of these flowers helps reframe the sorrow I associate with the day of my birth. For the first time, I see it as something worth celebrating. There was always a plan and I'm real. Known and chosen. The consolation prize, second best, last-one-picked-in-the-schoolyard role is nothing but a lie.

––––––––––

In *Abba's Child*,[30] Brennan Manning quotes from a section of John Eagan's *A Traveler Toward the Dawn: The Spiritual Journey* in which Eagan describes a conversation with his spiritual director. "Define yourself radically as one beloved by God"[31] the spiritual director tells Eagan. "God's love for you and his choice of you constitute your worth. Accept that, let it become the most important thing in your life."[32] These words resonated with Manning, the ragamuffin whose life was one of both deep sorrow and a blessed awareness of the boundless love and grace of God. They do with me too. I've experienced that radical love for myself and now I have a piece of paper proving I'm real. It's time to let go of what Manning calls my imposter self—the part of me that's preoccupied with gaining acceptance and approval and motivated by fear of not living up to the expectations of others. But beloved? Can I also learn to live as one who is beloved?

Chapter 8

DELIGHTS

It didn't take me long to learn that the discipline or practice of writing these essays occasioned a kind of delight radar. Or maybe it was more like the development of a delight muscle. Something that implies that the more you study delight, the more delight there is to study.

Ross Gay, *The Book of Delights*

I hear the words the cardiologist says, but it's the image of Gerry's heart with the main artery 90 percent blocked makes it real. Maybe that's why they give patients these packets of information. I flip to the image of his heart taken after they inserted the stent. *Thank you.* My husband is the most unlikely candidate to be lying in a hospital bed talking about blockages and vascular improvement clinics.

He's active and a leader with the local hiking club (he really enjoys hiking). He climbs mountains in the summer and snowshoes in the winter, has never smoked, is easygoing, eats a mostly plant-based diet, and doesn't have an immediate family history of heart disease. Yet here he is. Unlike my hospital stay a few years ago resulting in a diagnosis of stress, there's a physical reason for the discomfort Gerry experienced when hiking one afternoon.

Disbelief (gobsmacked—that's a good word to describe how we feel) turns to reality as we walk the corridors of the hospital hand-in-hand, getting enough activity to ensure all is well with the stent before they discharge him. We have a quiet conversation about a new normal and return to his room to watch the clock. A few minutes after noon—the appointed hour when the doctor said Gerry could leave—the nurse removes the tube in his arm and pronounces him sprung.

"Let's blow this popsicle stand," Gerry says.

He rises from the edge of the hospital bed and I tuck the information packet into my bag. Gerry bids farewell to his roommate and we walk out, eager to put this cardiac event behind us. My morning reading reminded me to trust in the one who loves us most and best. It's all we can do. I remind Gerry of the wisdom of resting and trusting as we walk toward the elevator.

———————

The reluctant patient struggles to curtail his activity. I suggest a visit to the vegetable garden to water and harvest greens for supper, followed by a walk through the nearby rose garden in the park where we sat four years earlier, eating sandwiches and deciding to return to Kamloops. We used to meet there for lunch before we moved to Washington. I'd pull into the parking lot next to Gerry's car, he'd climb out with sandwiches and cold drinks, and we'd head to the rose garden to eat and enjoy a respite in the middle of the day.

The fragrance of roses in the garden is heavenly. A woman dressed in a dark business suit strolls along the path opposite us. She pauses, lifts a flower to her nose, and indulges in aromatherapy in the middle of a busy workday. I remember how pockets of time like this revived me before I got too busy to take advantage of them. Now, I pray the wisdom of the pause is not lost on me—on us—ever again.

We walk, stopping at certain roses where Gerry shades the midday sun, and I capture images with my camera. We sit for a time on a bench and let the mid-September sun warm our bodies. I could sit for a good while more, but Gerry is restless. This "gradually easing back into regular activity" is challenging for him.

We take a meandering walk through the park toward the dock that was almost underwater in the spring flood season. Now it's almost autumn, and the river is low.

Nearby, geese rest on the shore and mallards glide in pairs under the dock. A young man wearing earbuds leans on the railing of the dock doing something on his phone. I want to grab him by the shoulders. *Look up! Pay attention! You only have a finite number of moments like this to enjoy. Don't waste them!* An older couple stands farther out on the dock. The woman points at something in the distance, and they both look out across the water. The gift of being present seems to come easier with age and the realization the days ahead are fewer than those behind.

"We should do this more often," I say.

In time, we walk back through the park toward the car. Stillness comes in many forms. I find it in solitude and silence, in the garden, when I'm writing, and when I'm capturing photos of the wonders of creation. My husband hears God's whisper when he's hiking on mountains. It's hard for him to be still in the way I choose, as it would be for me if I wanted to take part in the strenuous hikes he favours. One way isn't better than the other, they're just different—like we are. But we must remain flexible, and trust we can find stillness anywhere, because the divine isn't constrained by anything.

———————

The evening sky takes on the strangest hue around supper time. I grab my phone and head out to the deck to take a photo that doesn't come close to doing justice to the strange light. Others in the city pull out their DSLRs and are marginally more successful. Images of the evening sky pepper social media. One person doesn't even try—she posts a status update saying no photo can capture the wonder. She's the wisest one of all.

Before long, the sun sets, darkness falls, and I'm left with a lingering melancholy. The odd light seemed like a harbinger of something but now it's life as usual. Life is sweet in light of the past few months, but I am still hungry. The awe of many eyes turned upward at the evening sky and the small world I see through the macro lens of my camera are both facets of the awe of creation. They satisfy something, but not everything, because it's the Creator, more than the creation, I long for. And there's that word again—the one that's been tangled up in my mind for months: love. It's there in the sky's vastness and the tiniest flower petal; in the storm and the stillness; and walking through recovery from a cardiac event.

I challenge myself, as we head into the dark months again: keep your eyes on the Source of the dark and the light, the joy and the pain, the grace and the broken. Let go of everything else. Listen. Live as one beloved and fall into the arms of love.

———————

"I'm done with winter."

We're on the way to Vernon for our weekly visit with Gerry's mom and it's snowing. I play with the camera on my phone trying to capture an image reflecting my doneness.

"Did you just say you're done with winter?" Gerry turns toward me, grinning at the obvious: it's barely November and we've still got months of winter ahead of us.

Yes. I'm done. With winter arriving far too early, with waking up at 3:00 in the morning since we turned the clocks back to Standard Time, with the pain in my neck and shoulder caused by an uptick in computer time because of a malfunction I'm trying to fix by myself, with the headache I woke with this morning, and a mind working overtime. I'm done with it all. Maybe my doneness and I should have taken a solitude and silence day but life doesn't always allow such luxury.

Gerry drives on through snow that will seem pretty six weeks from now but that today is irritating. I open my window and try for another photo. Maya, from her spot in her special seat between us, glances my way at the sudden cold breeze but wisely keeps her counsel to herself.

Hours later we arrive back home. The snow still falls like dandruff. The worst of the early season storm bypassed our city, but the ground is white. I head to the kitchen to put the kettle on for tea while Gerry clears a space in the snow on the lawn for Maya (small dog parents will understand this). I'm tense and close to the edge.

"Oh good, you're making tea," Gerry comes into the kitchen to get a treat for Maya who has made good use of the cleared space on the lawn.

"Yes. I'm taking my tea down to my office and I don't want to be disturbed for an hour. Or more. Pretend I'm dead."

My husband, who tries to understand his wife's need for solitude, nods. He recognized the depth of my doneness and saw this coming. Pretend I'm dead, or PID as we say in shorthand. It was something we adopted during the years when I was writing *Two Hearts* and needed time alone to write. It's become one of those husband-wife things.

I take my phone and a cup of raspberry mojito green tea downstairs and flick on the stove in my office. Maya settles into her bed as I navigate to a playlist on my phone. A voice comes like velvet through the Bluetooth speaker on my desk. Music does the thing it does so well through the marriage of words of melody and I'm reminded I'm not alone on this sometimes-confusing often-painful path. I settle in at my desk and look out the picture window at the white outside. I feel done but solitude and writing will help. After a good night's sleep, I'll be back on track tomorrow. I write a few words and then head upstairs for the evening.

―――――――――

The current buzzword is *hygge*—the Danish concept of settling into home and appreciating simple and ordinary things. I used the word in an essay I contributed to an anthology and the editor wanted me to remove it and replace it with a word the reader would more easily understand. I resisted, and the word remained. Now everyone is talking about *hygge*. The season changes, fluffy socks and warm sweaters come out. We look for outward things to bring us inner peace. Stillness beckons.

Stillness—an overused word that has lost much of its meaning, but I can think of no better one to describe what I hunger for. I don't find it in images of hands at the end of sweatered arms wrapped around mugs of steaming tea, or in top-down photos of a streamlined white keyboard surrounded by pens and notebooks and reading glasses and an ever-present mug of hot tea. It's not dreamy images of a long-haired woman looking off in the distance. It's all these things, and it's none of these things.

Stillness is something I talk about but still struggle to practise. It's sitting with my Bible on my lap and my eyes closed, lost in conversation with God. It's sitting on the cool grass with my camera leaning in to photograph a sprig of lavender on a warm autumn afternoon. It's hands, warm and sudsy, washing breakfast dishes—a morning meditation that slows my pace. It's intentional, something to seek after, fall gently into, and rest. It's a memory and a hope; it's the meeting of eyes across a room connecting heart to holy heart. It's a whisper in the night.

———————————

Can you do it? Walk as though you're beloved? Can you embrace stillness in the middle of the busy? Can you walk taking your inherent value from the fact that you were created without the need to justify your worth?

I pose the questions to myself as I realize I've got commitments every day this week. I'm already feeling overwhelmed with lists and technology issues taking far too much of my attention. The day doesn't start out well, and I lose my tenuous grasp on peace early.

Then, delights show up.

Gerry and I sit in a coffee shop munching on turkey and stuffing sandwiches. I sip a frothy half-sweet caramel macchiato in between bites. We chat about this-and-that and it's a wonderful treat in the middle of the day. We finish our sandwiches and poke around for a while in the adjoining bookstore. It was once a special treat for me to steal away, grab a coffee, and spend an hour with books; it's been far too long since I indulged.

Then, we head to Gerry's appointment at the vascular improvement clinic and I lose my way in the city I've lived in since I was eighteen (save for those seven years we spent in Washington state). It would be comical if it weren't so frustrating. I wait for him in the car feeling discombobu-lated, tired, and fuzzy. Maybe I'm coming down with something. He returns, encouraged by an excellent report and amused by a nurse's reaction when she realizes he's seventy years old. I turn the car toward home, certain of the way this time. My phone dings with text messages and the car reads them to us. Amazing.

By the time we get home it's getting dark. It's only 3 pm, but this is December. Maya reminds us it's her supper time, Gerry feeds her, and I change into flannel pajamas and head down to my office to connect the external hard drive I picked up when we were out. The door is closed and inside, next to my desk, the faux wood stove hums. I smile in gratitude for my thoughtful husband who got there before me and turned it on so I'd be warm as I worked. I plug in the device and start the restore to retrieve data I lost, turn off the heater, and head back upstairs.

"Thank you for turning on the heater."

He knows I've felt burdened by my computer issues, his health concerns, and general December-ness. I know there is a point of diminishing return and sometimes we do more by doing less, but that truth is as difficult to embrace as it was for Gerry a few months ago. But it's the better way. Gerry draws me into his arms. I need to let myself pause for more of this. The heaviness of the day falls away and I allow it.

I sit on the floor and throw Maya's toy for a few rounds of fetch as we watch the news. In good time, I pull some things out of the fridge, thankful for an easy supper of leftovers requiring no effort to pull together. Evening passes.

We watch a favourite program on TV and I take a few trips downstairs to check on things and restart other things. I have a phone conversation, put a few drops of lavender essential oil in the diffuser, and fall into bed.

I open my eReader and read a few words, then switch to another book. I browse through the virtual library, but nothing holds my attention, so I put the device down, breathe a prayer of thanksgiving, and declare the day done. I didn't carry stillness with me throughout, but I cultivated pockets in the midst. That's something. It's more than I once was capable of.

———————

Another day.

We've been out for hours running errands and shopping. I drop Gerry off for his appointment at the vascular improvement clinic and head out to do some solitary December shopping that has to be done without a husband in tow.

The stores are busy. The streets are busy. Quickly, it ceases to be fun and, with my mission accomplished, I head back to wait for my husband. I pull into a parking space at the far end of the parking lot and am about to open the car door to make the trek toward the clinic but change my mind. Instead, I switch off the satellite radio that's morphed from music to noise somewhere along the way, close my eyes, and allow the sweet comfort of silence to do its work. I sit for about half an hour in the quiet, watching the odd person come and go but mostly refu-elling. In time, feeling sufficiently restored, I switch on a quiet Christmas album and the simple music—festive but not overpowering—eases me back.

Gerry is late from his appointment, but the extra time gives me an opportunity to regain my equilibrium. When he phones to tell me he's ready, I drive to the pickup area where he's standing outside waiting and hop out of the car as he tosses his bag in the back.

"You can drive. I'm done with traffic."

He pulls out onto the road and tells me about the appointment. There is cause for gratitude—for the clinic and the good report, medical intervention a few months ago, time we spent together earlier, for the pocket of silence, and even for stops we still have to make before we head for the sanctuary of home. There's always something. Gifts, delights—they're always there if I pay attention.

Early one morning, after the busyness of the season has passed, Gerry hands me a mug of soy milky frothy coffee.

"I can see the stars outside. That means the arctic front has moved in."

I'm not sure if that's a good thing or not. I think it means an end to the heavy snowfall yesterday. My husband has a cold. Essential oils and the cough syrup I made from peppermint leaves harvested from the garden are flowing.

He cancels hikes and we drag out quilts and books. It's not a bad way to spend the last darkest days of the year.

Wendell Berry, in his foreword to *Living the Sabbath: Discovering the Rhythms of Rest and Delight*, says the sabbath "invites us to stop. It invites us to rest. It asks us to notice while we rest, the world continues without our help."[33] So too, the trifecta sabbath of a cardiac event, a winter cold, and an arctic front moving in. Like a Sunday worship service, it invites us to "delight in the world's beauty and abundance."[34] and remember "the world will continue in our absence."[35]

Teach me.

I wake every morning with prayer winding through my mind. Two simple words acknowledging I don't know all the answers—the realization, both humbling and empowering. The older I get, the more I know I don't know and that's okay—it's good. That's wisdom. Enough for today, that's all I need. Moment by moment, hour by hour.

I make plans, set goals, and seek wisdom in walking them out. I ask questions, and can't hear the answers in the clamour, so take shelter and listen for love. And there it is—that whisper, that wisdom. Some questions remain but I am grounded in grace and given what I need to walk through one good day at a time.

Every time, you come through and I'm in awe.

Something almost magical happens as I see myself as beloved. I see those around me as equally beloved and realize the concept of *other* is where we get off track. We're not so different from each other. We're all a bit wounded. We lash out now and then from the sheer grief living in this world brings, but inside every one of us is an abundantly loved soul. It's a gradual unveiling but the more I believe in my own belovedness, the more I see it in others. Like the person who cut me off in traffic and the person I'm struggling in relationship with. And Mary.

I have so much peace since my great encounter and I want to go deeper. *Let this be the year the magic returns.*

Chapter 9

SATURATING

But when the words mean even more than the writer knew they meant, then the writer has been listening. And sometimes when we listen, we are led into places we do not expect, into adventures we do not always understand.

Madeleine L'Engle, *Walking on Water: Reflections on Faith and Art*

It's not yet six in the morning and I've been awake for a couple of productive hours. I stand at the window and look down into a backyard buried in pristine snow, unmarred by deer tracks or anything else, and see magic in the moonlight. The snow sparkles as if sprinkled with fairy dust like the snow of my prairie childhood. It's the snow I shuffled through, with frozen toes in too-small winter boots, on my way to school. It's the snow we fell into, waving arms and legs to make snow angels, that we waddled Charlie Chaplin-like in to make tractor tracks with our boot prints, and that made my wool mittens heavy with ice baubles. It's the snow I saw when I looked out our front room window on Christmas morning, convinced the wintery world had become enchanted throughout the silent, holy night. There was always something different about the way the snow-blanketed yard and street in front of our house looked on December 25th. I saw it well into adulthood. Then my world went dark, the magic left, and while I look for it every year, it's never been that way again. Now, I think if it wasn't so cold, I'd go outside and dance in it.

I tiptoe to the kitchen, pour soy milk into a glass, and put it in the microwave. As red numbers count down from seventy-seven and the Keurig coughs and spurts out elixir behind me, I pray. *Oh God, you have brought me in safety to this new day.*[36] That thing in my body that's been causing me trouble still burns, that concern in my heart for that person—no, persons—still weighs on me, and that other thing I've been procrastinating about still nags, but right here, right now, before the savage animals of the day come at me with teeth barred and low growls deep in their throat, I pause. *In all I do, direct me to the fulfilling of your purpose.*[37]

Yesterday, I saw a sparrow sitting on a branch of the leafless lilac tree in our backyard. There was something about the bird and the branches and I thought of the Creator. It was a sweet moment that passed like a whisper, one of those thin moments when heaven touches earth.

And now, here in the kitchen where the only light comes from the hydroponic garden where tiny blushing tomatoes grow and ripen, and the only sound comes from my practised steps as I prepare a perfect cup of morning coffee, I think of that tiny sparrow.

When the countdown gets to zero, I take the warm milk out of the microwave, froth it, and pour it into the cup of coffee. *You hear my simple prayers and grant me the sweetness of your presence.* I pad back to the bedroom with my mug of coffee in hand and Maya raises her tiny head. Her Yorkie eyes follow me. Gerry still slumbers. I set my coffee cup on the bedside table, climb back into bed, and reach for my tablet to tap out a few words. Day begins. *Have mercy.*

———————

January begins with intention, but intention is not the motivator I once believed it to be. It's a tool—a strong and useful one—but on its own, not enough to entice me to carve out a daily practice of solitude and silence. It will fall short without something more powerful to back it up. But fueled by love, intention fulfills its purpose. In the early morning, when all is quiet and fresh before I've messed anything up, love woos me. Nothing satisfies more than the time of sweet communion. Some mornings, it's as if the Creator sits down beside me, puts an arm around my shoulders, and says, "Daughter, I want to show you something." I understand a deeper level of love. Like Lewis, my first business of the day is to push aside savage things so I can listen "to that other voice . . . letting that other larger, stronger, quieter life come flowing in"[38] and fan into flame the truth I glimpsed in the great encounter.

Once, accounts of those who spoke of loving God mystified me. My faith was mostly an act of will. I prayed, remained faithful in my devotion, served when opportunity presented, and hoped it would be enough. I was mystified by a story someone told who described a sense of "liquid love" pour over her at a time of personal encounter. I wasn't at all certain I loved or was loved. But something shifted, beginning with an encounter behind French doors and culminating one spring morning when I saw clear, deeply personal, life-altering truth. I understood my belovedness. In the moment of understanding, I could do nothing but love in return. It's been that way since.

———————

I write through ideas that could turn into something of substance, but I try not to get too far ahead of myself. I come to the page, first, to listen. Fear tries to stop me. The biggest, and loudest animal growls, "What will everyone think?" But love gives me permission, requiring and equipping me to keep moving. I've wished for most of my adult life that I was gifted with the ability to speak with confidence and that I wasn't introverted and awkward. I've been given a measure of competence with the written word and relish times of solitude when I can use it to wrestle through difficult and delicious things. Ever since I learned to hold a pencil, I've formed letters into words, words into sentences, then stories, and even a book. Writing helped me navigate the precarious path of adolescence. It helped keep me afloat when my world went dark. It returned, like a wise old friend, to guide me when it was time to go deeper. Writing is as much a part of me as breathing. Perhaps I struggle with the spoken word because my native language is the written word. I'm overwhelmed in large groups of people. I'm better with one-on-one interaction but, even then, I have a propensity to trip over my words. Maybe it's selfish to wish for the ability to navigate social situations with adeptness and charm in addition to having the gifts of introversion and contemplation. Introversion a gift? I'm seeing it, and the ability to think deep thoughts and rumi- nate on truth as gifts.

My life's work is to write. It's an idea I haven't put into words before but tapping them out on the keyboard gives it credence. What if my social anxiety and the path I've walked, coupled with a modest ability to wrangle words positions me uniquely to touch the heart of one person? Or what if, through the process of writing, I myself am transformed and the intersection of my life with another accomplishes a purpose? Why would I choose to not do that? What if I stopped lamenting what I don't have and cultivated and cared for what I do have, then used it for the benefit of others? Isn't that enough? Maybe more than enough—a calling? It's a heady thought.

Wise author Madeleine L'Engle says "Of course. It's all been said better before. If I thought I had to say it better than anyone else, I'd never start."[39] If she struggled to come to the page every day, is there any reason I shouldn't likewise? I'm not competing with Madeleine or anyone else. "We each have to say it, to say it in our own way. Not of our own will, but as it comes through us. Good or bad, great or little: that isn't what human creation is about. It's that we have to try; to put it down in pigment, or words, or musical notation, or we die."[40]

I serve a few reasonable words on my blog every morning. I tap out thoughts and prayers in my private journal and words help me sort through the muck, clearing my vision so I can see the treasure. I release the idea of writing another book. I let go of the idea I have to do anything with photography other than enjoy the creative process of capturing images of the wonder of creation. Prayer becomes meditation and I listen. The driving need to find significance in anything other than the gift of my life is gone.

———————

The loss of my birth mother catapulted me into grief. For you, it was probably something else. We all carry a measure of it. We struggle to articulate it but in silence and solitude where no distractions keep us from it, grief bubbles to the surface and demands we pay attention. We don't like it because it hurts, so we do the work we need in order to heal or, if we're not yet ready, look for something to ease the ache. We find a behaviour, substance, or something else to keep us from feeling—busyness did it for me. It helps for a while, but we must come to terms with what haunts us if we're to grow and mature and keep from passing our pain on.

Physician and expert on childhood development, trauma, and addiction, Gabor Mate says, "Passion creates; addiction consumes—first the self and then others within its orbit."[41] Passion for our work and creative pursuits causes us to go all in. We study, practise, enthusiastically improve our craft, and create something new—like a photograph or story, a project plan or computer program. It's good. I was all in with my career and subsequent retirement focus on gardening and canning—on the surface, there was nothing wrong with any of it. But when numbing becomes the thing we crave most of all, we slip into over-doing or over-consuming and fall headlong into addiction. I learned to value numbing above all else. I didn't like feeling abandoned or rejected by the woman who was supposed to love me most of all. I told myself I understood her plight but it didn't ease my pain. Going and doing became my addiction and kept me from feeling it. Accolades became my payoff and justified my being.

We don't get too far into addiction before there's little left with which to relate healthily toward others, or flow in creativity meant to be an outlet of the beautiful gifts given us. Going and doing and numbing inhibited my ability to function creatively. It's why I struggled with abstract photography prompts and sat empty and uninspired at my writing desk. Living real asks of us that which is most difficult: to face headlong into our pain, feel it, and then release it. It's the most terrifying thing we can do. It's also the most generous. And it frees us.

There have been seasons when I struggled to hold on. After the death of my first marriage when I first came face-to-face with grief over the loss of my first mother, my families of origin, and the dream upon which I had built a shaky foundation with my then-husband, my curled fingers slipped, my line of vision narrowed and I, Kilroy-like, slid imperceptibly lower and lower. My faith was barely able to keep me from falling into the abyss. I laid wide awake at night begging an unseen and unfelt God to do the kindest thing: to take me home. I felt unworthy of anything else. The fact was every single person who came into my life left, confirming my insignificance. Like George Bailey in the Christmas classic, *It's a Wonderful Life*, I wished I had never been born.

I prayed, even though it felt like my prayers hit the ceiling and fell dead and worthless to the ground beside me. I struggled to believe in a God who loved me, and I wondered if I loved him in return. In time I came through, arriving at a place of gratitude and understanding, and delight came into my life as I embarked on a new trajectory.

I stood with my hands raised and eyes closed singing to an audience of one, feeling a measure of love rise in my praise. Other times, I clung to my faith though I felt nothing. I hungered for experience, but believed experience wasn't necessary. God, in his grace, told me otherwise.

Love changed everything when, in the still and secret place, and in the way I'm crafted to understand best, I heard a whisper. No longer Kilroy, struggling to hold on and catch a glimpse of something elusive, I let go as only one who knows they are beloved can, and fell into the arms of the one who loved me first and who still loves me best. Now, with love fueling my intention I spend time in silence and solitude, praying and listening, being present, and seeing the divine in ordinary things like a sparrow on a barren lilac branch.

Once, when I was a young mom, I contracted the September flu, which takes up residence in homes every year when kids return to school. It was a tough one that year, and it laid me out. In my weakened state, desperate for relief, I went along with the advice of someone who insisted I take copious amounts of aspirin. Instead of feeling better, I got worse. I dragged my sick self to the doctor, who agreed the aspirin was making me sicker and advised me to stop taking it.

"You have to saturate the tissues," he told me. "Stop taking aspirin and drink plenty of liquids."

There was something about the concept of saturating the tissues that made sense. Armed with my doctor's advice, I ignored the well-meaning, but misguided, advice and stopped swallowing the pills and consumed liquids instead. I became saturated, and I got better. It's like that now. I'm saturated with love, all is exceedingly well,[42] and I'm getting better.

Chapter 10

FALLOW

There is a pervasive form of modern violence to which the idealist . . . most easily succumbs: activism and overwork. The rush and pressure of modern life are a form, perhaps the most common form, of its innate violence. To allow oneself to be carried away by a multitude of conflicting concerns, to surrender to too many demands, to commit oneself to too many projects, to want to help everyone in everything is to succumb to violence. The frenzy of the activist neutralizes his (or her) work . . . It destroys the fruitfulness of his (or her) work, because it kills the root of inner wisdom which makes work fruitful.

Thomas Merton

One day I'm behind an older couple in the lineup at the grocery store. She, kind-faced and smiling, bundled up in a dated tweed coat with a knitted hat on top of her head, lifts packed plastic bags and puts them in the cart. He is preoccupied with scrutinizing prices on the screen as their items are scanned. When the clerk reaches the end of their order and announces the final tally, the man fumbles for his wallet as if it hadn't occurred to him before he would have to transact business before taking the groceries home. He counts out a few bills, squints at the total on the screen, and digs in his pocket for a few coins to make the correct change.

I'm in no hurry. His slow pace is both amusing and calming in the middle of a busy afternoon spent running errands. The wife glances over at me and smiles as if to say *I'm sorry*. I smile back. *No problem.* The clerk hands him a receipt and the old man stuffs his wallet into his back pocket and shuffles toward the door behind his buggy-pushing wife.

"Retired people," the grocer says, shaking his head. "Nothing to do and all day to do it."

I don't think he's much younger than me (or maybe he is, I have a skewed perception of my age in relation to other people) but he seems to have no appreciation for the wisdom of advancing years and for being present that these dear ones bring. How many others are like him? No wonder I struggle with finding significance now that I have nothing to do and all day to do it. (I didn't get the memo on this, by the way.)

A reminder popped up on my calendar this morning: it's been four years since I walked out of the office and shed the title of Business Analyst. I still stumble when someone asks what I do. "I'm retired." There must be a better word. Reimagined? Or better yet, *jubilación*. Isabel Allende, in a TED Talk[43] about living with passion, spoke of the Spanish word for retirement: *Jubilación*. Translated, it means celebration. "I don't have to prove anything anymore,"[44] says Allende. "I have chosen to stay passionate with an open heart and I'm working on it every day."[45] That seems a better description of what I left the corporate world to pursue.

After a dry spell lasting most of the past four years, I'm writing. I spend slow, meditative time capturing images in photographs for no other reason than to enjoy the process. I toss tiny seeds in the ground and tend plants that teach me about the way life works. I preserve the harvest to feed us during the dark months. But the way I do these things has changed. It's no longer busy work done to keep my body and mind occupied so I don't have to feel the things that are uncomfortable. It's slipped into the realm of creativity. *Jubilación*.

Once, I saw a television program where the host asked guests at the end of an interview to speculate on the reason we are here—our purpose. Interviewees gave many answers depending on their belief system. I shook my head at every response. No, that's not it. You're missing it. But I didn't have words to express what I knew in the deepest part of myself.

Now I see our purpose has nothing to do with the role we play at work, or whether we have enough things and activity with which to fill our days. We're created with a unique tapestry of gifts and we fulfill our purpose when we use them, joyfully, to serve good things to those whose lives intersect with ours. "The important thing is to recognize that our gift, no matter the size, is indeed something given us, for which we can take no credit, but which we may humbly serve,"[46] says Madeleine L'Engle. In doing so, we honour the Creator who gave them to us. Our lives become worship. We learn to love. It's that simple, and it's that complicated.

A handful of individuals have had a life-altering influence on my life, not because they had a title or tried to be something other than who they were. They lived one good day at a time, got up every morning and went to work (or stayed home to work), did a job well and with integrity, treated people with dignity and respect, and stood strong in their convictions. They created something beautiful: a poem, a photograph, a welcoming space, or a department at work everyone wanted to be a part of. They did the hard work of peacemaking rather than taking the easy path of keeping the peace at all cost to avoid conflict. They saw me, and everyone else as individuals. We all want to be seen and for someone like me who has felt invisible for most of her life, it's a most precious gift. These people weren't afraid to call me out when I needed to be called out. They acknowledged, and were profoundly thankful for, the grace in which they lived. They modelled the kind of person I wanted to be.

Whether we're chatting with a clerk at the grocery store, giving a presentation in a meeting, writing a blog post, painting a picture, tending a garden, taking a photograph, making a quilt, or cleaning our bathroom, we change the world when we live one good day at a time and use our gifts for the benefit of others and in honour of the one who gave them. Books, music, and art crafted by those who have not forgotten the way to wonderland are glimpses into our hearts' desire but they are not our hearts' desire. They "betray us if we trust them"[47] says Lewis because the beauty is "not in them, it only came through them, and what came through them was longing. These things—the beauty, the memory of our own past—are good images of what we really desire; but if they are mistaken for the thing itself they turn into dumb idols, breaking the hearts of their worshipers. For they are not the thing itself; they are only the scent of a flower we have not found, the echo of a tune we have not heard, news from a country we have never yet visited."[48]

―――――――

It feels like it has always been winter. The days are grey. Snow and rain; rain and snow. It wears on me and I grow impatient. I celebrated when I saw the first crocus poking up its tentative purple head in my flower bed. Now, there's ice-encrusted snow everywhere and the brave little flower is buried underneath. Our street is a mess of frozen ruts. It's easier to stay at home. I'm grateful for my well-stocked pantry so we don't have to go out.

I limit my exposure to the news and social media because it feels too much like assault amid the grey. The anger, name-calling, and hypocrisy is hard to bear any time, especially so in the dark months. Madeleine L'Engle says: "Like it or not, we either add to the darkness of indifference and out-and-out evil which surrounds us or we light a candle to see by."[49] I try to light candles with words and photographs—even mason jars filled with jewel-like tomatoes shine a certain light when I pull one off the shelf to make dinner. We all know the candle is the better choice but sometimes we struggle to find a match with which to light one. So, we sit in the dark, our eyes grow accustomed to the shadows, and in our blindness we reach our empty hands into the blackness. We pull back in fear or swipe at nothing when our hands brush against something unknown. Finally, we realize there has been a match in our hand all along, we strike it, and see the unseen threat was really no threat at all.

If only the trajectory toward spring continued in a straight line. If only progress on our life plans was always predictable and steady. But it doesn't, and it's not, and we learn to adapt, and embrace the wait. We pull out seed catalogues and dream of spring.

———————

I wake in the middle of another long, cold night. The room is chilly, despite the hum of the furnace. I'm thankful for flannel and the warm body of my husband and a Yorkie curled up next to me. I pray for a while, then reach for my eReader and *The Imitation of Christ*. Kempis asks: "What doth it profit to argue about hidden and dark things, concerning which we shall not be even reproved in the judgement, because we knew them not?"[50] I wonder if he looked into the future and saw a world where social media created monsters of us toward one another.

"Oh, grievous folly, to neglect the things which are profitable and necessary, and to give our minds to things which are curious and hurtful!"[51] Wisdom tells us to pay more heed to the better thing. We hurt others and ourselves when we pay too much mind to the dark things.

"The more a man hath unity and simplicity in himself, the more things and the deeper things he understandeth; and that without labour, because he receiveth the light of understanding above."[52] The clamour of the marketplace, even back in the twelfth century, was prone to distract from the more important work of listening.

Sleep returns and I rest well, my burden lightened.

Later I wake from a dream in which I was gardening to find snow falling again. The sense of having spent time in the garden is sweet. Anticipating doing it again soon is pleasing. But for now, it's still winter.

A reader leaves the words "lying fallow and being present" in a comment on my blog after I describe the January feeling that's dragging me down, as a slump. To her, it's a season of embracing the opportunity to rest. There's something about the phrase that rings true to me. It's my gentle companion throughout the day, and it lingers in my mind as I settle in to read at night. I look it up in an online dictionary.

Fallow: adj. 1. (of land) left unseeded after being ploughed and harrowed to regain fertility for a crop. 2. (of an idea, state of mind, etc.) undeveloped or inactive but potentially useful.[53]

As a gardener, I know the importance of crop rotation and feeding the soil, and that farmers will leave a piece of land fallow for a season. Neglecting these practices results in undernourished soil and an unproductive garden or crop. Failing to factor in a personal season of lying fallow can have a similar impact. It's what happened to me during the mind-numbing years working in an office. It's still easy to allow my focus to shift from being to doing. Did the phrase capture my attention because I've become too busy again? Have I lost sight of delight in simple things? Lying fallow. It sounds a lot like wisdom.

We're barely past the middle of February, the shortest month that seems to last for an eternity. My yearning for spring is so strong it aches. The days are longer, and a smattering of sunny days helps combat the insidious winter blahs, but then a blizzard blows in and a crazy amount of snow falls and keeps falling. The wind whips it into white whirls that dance all day. Gerry pulls on his winter gear and goes outside to shovel multiple times before the snow gets too heavy. I stay indoors and pull jars of canned soup from the shelf for lunch. We're snowed in until a snowplough comes. Thirty-three days until spring officially arrives— it's so close I can feel dirt on my hands and taste the first spinach salad of the season. *I think I can. I think I can.*

I spend a good part of the day alone in my office with my camera and in the company of words. The only sounds are the hum of the heater and the low drone of the essential oil diffuser on the corner of my desk. Maya pads in to check up on me. She hops up on the loveseat and takes a short nap, then curls up in front of the heater and naps again. My focus is on a fading bunch of Gerber daisies I arrange in front of the north-facing picture window. The light reflecting from the snow is lovely, highlighting shadows and the charm of drooping petals. I work slowly: capturing a few shots, repositioning the vase and my camera, and taking a few more. When I've exhausted angles, light, and perspective I move to my get-stuff-done desk to download and edit the images.

Later, I scratch out a draft for an article about first-of-the-year motivation. I write about being saturated with grace and changed by boundless love, and how these things work together to spark intention. I write about looking for the divine in the ordinary and finding fresh ways to write timeless truth. Something germinates as I write, and I wind up with a piece I can use.

———————

I'm on my way home from prayer, weary and thinking about a botanical garden near where we lived in Washington state, and wishing I could go there. It would be raining, not snowing, and I could walk amidst the green (oh, the Pacific Northwest green!) and feel my soul soothed. But, there's nothing like that in Kamloops and, even if there was, it would be under the cover of snow and ice at this time of year. An alternative comes to mind. I take a sharp left.

I walk through the front doors into the nursery like a weary traveller returning home. I carry on through the floral department where I admire rose bouquets leftover from Valentine's Day and other colourful floral arrangements. But they are not my destination. I make my way past the clothing department (why is there a clothing department in a garden shop?) and see everything is marked down to half price. Another sign of the looming change of seasons.

Then, there it is—an open glass door welcoming me into the greenhouse. Even in its late-winter disarray, filled with garden décor, tools, and hot tubs instead of plants, it's lovely. I wander up and down the aisles of tropical plants, admiring the beauty of the offerings. These few minutes in the middle of an ordinary day are an opportunity to give myself a quiet gift and make a statement I'm worthy to receive it. On the surface, it looks like nothing special: an ordinary looking woman browsing rows of plants in a nursery. In the unseen realm it's something altogether different. How many extraordinary things do we pass by every day without even noticing?

When I've seen it all—and it doesn't take long—I return to the main store and head to the gardening section. There's already an impressive array of seeds on display, and one day soon I'll lose myself there as I plan this year's garden. But today the siren call of the greenhouse bids me to return. I pick up a houseplant, consider buying it, but put it back on the shelf. A tropical plant on my windowsill won't delight me in the same way being in this place does. I wander, lost in thought, past plants and garden whimsy and, for now, it is enough.

———————

One day, when I'm letting Maya out to tend to her morning business, I feel warmth between the inside front door and the screen. My Yorkie makes a beeline for the grassy section of the lawn that grows larger every day as snow continues to melt. She sniffs, seeking precisely the perfect spot. As I wait, my eye catches a tiny splash of colour in the flower bed next to the house. The brave little crocus survived the late-winter storms after all. Maya trots toward the door. I let her in, grab my camera, and head back outside to capture some images of the little purple harbinger of spring.

On an afternoon in early March I open the garage door and set up a work area in the sunshine. It's a perfect day, the warmest one so far this year. I can't wait any longer. I drag a bag of seed starting mix to my workspace, bend forward, and inhale the aroma of hope. Nothing smells better at this time of the year than soil. The sweet smell, coupled with sunshine and melting snow, is bound to turn cabin fever into spring fever. I scoop seed starter into a large bucket, pour warm water over it, and reach in with a garden glove-clad hand to massage it. I work slowly and mindfully, enjoying the aromatherapy. The work I do is less a task to be crossed off a project plan and more a gift to myself. Gardening feeds me. It teaches timeless truth and the most important lessons come when I slow down and pay attention. I started to understand it when I tended my first little four-foot-by-four-foot raised bed back in Washington, but I lost sight of the truth along the way.

When the soil and water are one, I scoop handfuls of the damp earth into each of twelve little pots. I choose a white plastic stick labelled *Brandywine* and reach for the matching seed packet. I sprinkle three tiny seeds into my hand, drop the seed trio into the pot (only the strongest will ultimately survive), cover them with a dusting of potting mix, and insert the stick label. I repeat the process until I've planted six varieties of tomatoes, three kinds of peppers, and Genovese basil. Then, I carry the pots into the house and cover them with plastic wrap to create tiny individual greenhouses I place on warming mats. They'll live here, in my laundry room, until it's warm enough to transplant the seedlings outside in the garden.

Gardening at this early stage is an act of faith. Every year, I'm struck by the miracle that one of these tiny seeds will become a plant taller than me, providing us with delicious heirloom tomatoes well into autumn. Who in their left logical mind could believe it? "'It always amazes me to look at the little, wrinkled brown seeds and think of the rainbows in 'em,'"[54] says Captain Jim in Lucy Maud Montgomery's *Anne's House of Dreams*. "'When I ponder on them seeds I don't find it nowise hard to believe that we've got souls that'll live in other worlds. You couldn't hardly believe there was life in them tiny things, some no bigger than grains of dust, let alone colour and scent, if you hadn't seen the miracle, could you?'"

No indeed, Captain Jim. Miracles in this world and souls that will live in other worlds: sometimes I can scarce believe it myself. But year after year the gift of the garden reminds me of both miracles up close and those I believe in only through faith. The wisdom coming from tending a garden is plenty. We're heading into the season of learning and it all starts with these tiny seeds.

PART 3
Beloved

Chapter 11

DREAMING

There are times we dream our way to a truth or an insight so overwhelming that it startles us awake and haunts us for years to come.

Frederick Buechner, *Whistling in the Dark*

I'm wide awake. It's dark and, aside from the comforting hum of the furnace, the only sounds are steady cadence of sleep-breathing coming from Gerry beside me and Maya at the foot of the bed. There's no sleep left in me. Should I reach for my eReader or close my eyes and try to will myself back to sleep? I read of a strategy a respected writer uses to deal with sleepless nights: instead of going down the rabbit hole of overthinking he spends the time contemplating the character of God. No petitions, no requests, just quiet reflection. It seems like time well spent.

My thoughts go to the garden: the magic found in the miracle of seeds, companion planting, harvest, and how none of it happens by accident. *Master gardener.* Then the flowers in my front yard, and the wonder I see when I sit on the grass and look through the macro lens on my camera. There's an entire world there that, most of the time, I walk past unaware. *Unseen but here beside me.* And the vastness of the skies, blue and bright or black and starry—*multi-faceted and multi-dimensional*—and suddenly it's too much. Something happens and I imagine, as much as I dare, what it must be like for the Creator to behold a creation reflecting such glory.

I see a dull and muted diamond in the rough and watch as cuts are made revealing facets of light. The diamond is us. The cuts are the pruning and the pain as life chips away. We are hurt and cracked, but we're also polished and cleaned until prisms of light radiate from us. I imagine glimmers as faith overcomes darkness and turns into worship. I realize I'm smiling, overcome with joy, and there's that sense of being loved again.

———————

With increasing frequency, in the dark and solitary night season, I catch glimpses of things I can't hold on to or explain. I linger in a not-quite-awake-but-not-quite-asleep space, reluctant to let go. People alive only in my heart, places I haven't been to for a lifetime, if ever, and seasons long past but still present in my memory, wrap me in bittersweet. I try to hold on, realizing whatever it was is already starting to fade. Sometimes, later in the day, the memory slips from my subconscious and I almost weep from the longing.

C.S. Lewis used the German word, *sehnsucht* to describe the inconsolable longing for something we are unable to name. I think I've felt it for my entire life. Part melancholy, part joy, *sehnsucht* touches us in the deepest, most precious place. "Such longing is in itself the very reverse of wishful thinking: it is more like thoughtful wishing,"[55] says Lewis. Thoughtful wishing. Yes, that's it.

Madeleine L'Engle wrote of something *sehnsucht*-like, too. We're "all strangers in a strange land, longing for home, but not quite knowing what or where home is."[56] She says we "glimpse it sometimes in our dreams, or as we turn a corner, and suddenly there is a strange, sweet familiarity that vanishes almost as soon as it comes."[57] I've hungered all my life for that feeling of home. It's been so elusive.

Sehnsucht comes in the feel of the warm summer wind on my arms, in the smell of Jergens hand lotion, or the taste of a fresh-picked tomato on a white bread sandwich. It came when I worked alone in my kitchen crowded with memories. It comes in my dreams and it comes out of nowhere. There's no way to sweep it away. It lingers, bittersweet both in presence and absence. I lose myself in longing for something I can't articulate in a melancholy place of what-if and if-only where whispers of elusive things compress my heart.

Then this.

I dream I'm walking along a beach. It's dark—not night, but like night. Black and angry clouds fill the sky. Waves so large that I feel miniature in comparison crash on the beach. It's raining but I walk along the seashore without getting wet. The roar of the storm is the only thing I hear. It's deafening. I'd be terrified in real life, but in the dream the opposite is true. The roar comforts me. I have a sense I could scream my throat raw into the storm and it would absorb my pain. With the realization comes an understanding the sense of rejection and abandonment I've carried for almost sixty years can be, if not removed, at least understood, and I'll be loved in a way I've never been before. All I have to do is release it.

I stand head-on facing toward the raging sea as waves crash and wind whips, and I cry out into the storm. I rail against a broken woman who was not strong enough to keep her children. I howl about a man, broken himself, unwilling or unable to change, who broke others. I moan, tired from trying for so many years to fill a vessel leaking so slowly I don't even realize when it's nearing empty. I weep for all I have lost, the mistakes I have made, the things done to me, and the pain I caused others. As soon as the pain comes out of my throat, it's absorbed by the storm. I keep wailing until it's all out and I'm left with peace in the void left behind. Then I stand silent, eyes closed and arms outstretched, as I am filled.

———————

I'm different after having that dream. It's as if the love I felt for the first time when God used scripture to penetrate my crusty exterior and give me a sense of all-encompassing love now touches the deepest part of me. I don't know why, or how, or anything other than ineffable love. Augustine called it the "sweetness." Kate Bowler, professor of Christian history at Duke Divinity School, describes a sweet communion with God she felt when she was battling incurable stage four cancer. The feeling stayed for months. "In fact," she says, "I had grown so accustomed to that floating feeling that I started to panic at the prospect of losing it."[58] She asked around to see if any of her friends or colleagues had experienced something similar. Some had, others read about it. They all said the same thing. "Yes, it will go. The feelings will go. The sense of God's presence will go. There will be no lasting proof that God exists. There will be no formula for how to get it back."[59] I'm in the throes of it now and I can't fathom losing the feeling, though I fear it. I soak in the sweetness and trust when it goes, *if it must go*, I too will "somehow be marked by the presence of an unbidden God"[60] and changed. Bowler's friends told her the experience isn't proof of anything, it's simply a gift. What a gift it is.

Martin Luther wrote of prayers where "the heart speaks more than the mouth"[61] and said "those who pray least, seem to pray most."[62] Sure enough, my prayers, like those of Wendell Berry's *Jayber Crow*, dwindle "down nearer and nearer to silence."[63] Words seem inadequate. Like Jayber, "Lying awake at night, I could feel myself being changed—into what, I had no idea."[64] I wrestle, no longer only asking questions but being changed by them, and find solid and comfortable footing. I build a framework, through a liturgy of psalms and prayers saints have prayed for hundreds of years, in what I imagine as concentric circles taking me deeper to a safe place where personal prayers rise like fragrant offerings from the beloved to the Lover.

It will be years before I read Sarah Bessey's words (perhaps years before she writes them), but when I do, I find they echo my truth: "Prayer became less solitary and more communal . . . I drew comfort from the cloud of witnesses all praying these prayers together, at the same time, passing the prayers from hour to hour to one another like a torch in an Olympic relay race. . . . in these prayers, I borrowed the faith of those who still believed, even if we would not meet in this life."[65]

From solitude springs hunger for community, not as an organization or a means to fill a personal need but as a way of being in this world. Henri Nouwen teaches us why one precedes the other: "If we do not know we are the

THE PRESENCE OF ABSENCE

beloved sons and daughters of God, we're going to expect someone in the community to make us feel that way. They cannot."[66] At the start of our journey, we don't understand all humans will eventually disappoint us. We are all hurt, and as a result, we hurt others—not intentionally, but the wound is the same whether intentional or not. It's a cycle of pain that's perpetuated until something profound changes it. My own broken self won't be healed exclusively by connection with my original family. The first and most important thing to grasp is my status as beloved.

"I am the beloved, you are the beloved; together we can build a home"[67] says Nouwen. "We all have wounds. We are in so much pain. It's precisely this feeling of loneliness that lurks behind all our successes, that feeling of uselessness that hides under all the praise, that feeling of meaninglessness even when people say we're fantastic—that is what makes us sometimes grab onto people and expect from them an affection and love they cannot give."[68] In Nouwen's words I see my wounding and hunger for significance is not uncommon. Mine springs from the loss of my first mother's love, but there's some disquieting thing in all of us trying to make us believe we're unworthy. Through the truth of our belovedness comes healing.

Nouwen says true "community is not loneliness grabbing onto loneliness . . . It's solitude grabbing onto solitude."[69] Solitude teaches us not to expect a utopian existence where nothing goes amiss and we love one another well. We come to understand we won't feel loving or loved all the

time because this world is simply not capable of allowing it.
 So, we learn to forgive, and it equips us to remain faithful
to our community. We seek, and find, unconditional and
relentless love in the Divine and then we can forgive tres-
passes, see one another as beloved, and celebrate the gifts
each individual brings to the community. We begin to
heal—ourselves and one another—and find we're not so
different after all. Grounded in solitude and silence, we go
out into the world and share the gift of ourselves without
comparing either our portion or contribution.

The virtual companionship of other contemplative
souls affirms I'm not the only one to wrestle this way.
Some scratched out thoughts hundreds of years ago, others
amidst the din of modern times. Some seek fulfillment of a
holy longing; others instinctively seek sanctuary in stillness
though they can't say why.

The psalmist reminds me of strength I find in quiet
and confidence.[70] Augustine writes of God caring "for each
one of us as though [we are] the only one."[71] In Wm. Paul
Young's beautiful book, *The Shack*, Papa speaks of those
she is "especially fond of"[72]—and this seems to be the
most profound truth of all. I'm not blind to the fact that if
"Auggie" and Paul were to sit across a table in a coffee shop
discussing the fine points of their theology, they would
uncover more than a few differences. That they both experienced the sweetness and understood that *beloved* isn't a
title reserved only for those who camp in their exclusive
park, makes me belive they'd see past theological differ-

ences to the belovedness inherent in the other. I wish more of us could do the same.

May Sarton opens her *Journal of a Solitude* saying, "I am here alone for the first time in weeks, to take up my 'real' life again at last. That is what is strange—that friends, even passionate love, are not my real life unless there is time alone in which to explore and to discover what is happening or has happened."[73] But, she says "without the interruptions . . . life would become arid." She understood the gift of community and the wisdom in drawing away from the crowd for a time of contemplation. For her, like me, life without solitude overwhelms.

"The world calls them its singers and poets and artists and story-tellers,"[74] writes Lucy Maud Montgomery of those who have "never forgotten the way to fairyland."[75] When we creatives risk being vulnerable, and share the deepest part of ourselves through something we create, we open the door to someone else understanding they're not alone.

C.S. Lewis talks about the sense of companionship that occurs when we realize we "have in common some insight or interest or even taste which the others do not share and which, till that moment, each believed to be his own unique treasure (or burden)."[76] We form a bond. We realize we're not alone. We "stand together in an immense solitude."[77]

I'm prone to seek an immediate, albeit temporary, soothing of my personal pain but I see the balm is never in quick fixes or the world's definition of the so-called sweet life. It's always and forever found in the healing presence of the Divine and, for me in this season, it comes through silence and solitude.

———————

It's grey again. Spring's return is so gradual this year, and every rare day the sun shines is cause for celebration. There's blue sky and sunshine somewhere above the grey; nothing can stop the change of seasons. The sun breaks through around noon, and I take advantage of the break to head to the community garden. A light rain falls while I'm driving. I turn the wipers on with stubborn determination. *I don't care. I'm gardening.*

The drizzle has stopped by the time I unlock the gate and walk the path toward my plot, with trowel and seed packets in my hand. I survey the space, imagining it full of produce in a few months, before laying out rows and dropping tiny radish, lettuce, and kale seeds in the furrows. There's not much else to do. It starts to rain again so I don't stay long, but the garden has done its work. I come away fed.

———————

Weeks later I stand at the edge of my garden with a hose, directing a gentle spray and scanning the soil for signs of life. I spy pea and radish shoots but there's no sign of kale, lettuce, or the extra row of spinach I sowed when I worried my fall-planted spinach wasn't as far along as my neighbour's. It's the same thing every year. I worry my garden will be a bust, but before long we're enjoying her bounty and marvelling at the day-to-day growth. She'll feed us well through the summer, I'll tuck her gifts in the freezer and on the canning shelf, and a half year from now I'll be tired of the whole thing and ready to let both the garden and my weary self lie fallow for the winter.

This worry every spring is ridiculous—a waste of time and energy—yet no matter how often I set myself straight, there remains a spark of concern that my seeds won't germinate or that we didn't amend the soil enough, and my plot will be barren. Experience tells me that this space where the only thing of any significance growing right now is fall-planted garlic and the odd persistent weed will transform into a lush and beautiful bed of life in a few months. I struggle to believe it, even though I've seen it come to pass year after year.

This little plot of land where I coax vegetables to life teaches me so much. Here, as in life, I walk by faith. What I see isn't always a good predictor of what is to come. Patience yields a reward. There is wisdom in the practices of self-discipline and delayed gratification. There's so much more to it than busy work when I pay attention.

Some things in the garden won't turn out as I'd wish (like the yellow turnips I planted last year; they never amounted to much and I won't plant them again), but others will delight (last year was an excellent one for radishes). If rodents eat the root crops and the cucumbers are misshapen, the tomatoes will be plentiful and the peppers fat and juicy. All it will take is a little more sunshine and a few more warm days and things will start happening. The garden will grow as it should—a little different every year—but all in good time. I don't know what it will look like, but I know enough for today. If that's not an illustration of a faith-directed life I don't know what is. I'm determined, this year, to enjoy the experience of tending my garden rather than becoming overwhelmed with the busyness of it.

———————

"What a lovely sight," Gerry says. Sarcasm drips, as he pulls back the curtains in the bedroom. "Snow on the top of the hills."

I have a sore throat and a stuffy head—it's been years since I had a cold and one takes hold now when I should be out in the garden enjoying the non-existent sunshine. It's insulting. I turn toward the window and, sure enough, there's a dusting of snow atop the hills across the valley like vanilla frosting on a cupcake. It's April. And it's so wrong. At least the stuff falling outside our window isn't white. Liquid sunshine: that's what we called it when we lived in the Pacific Northwest where it rained, and rained, and rained even more. I'd take rain over snow in April given a choice.

The grey these past weeks has left me unmotivated to write and with little inspiration to bring out my Canon. I wait, like I'm parched and watching for a drop of water to fall from a rusty tap, until I can't stand it any longer. I grab my camera and take my barefoot self out into the back yard. The grass is cold on my feet as I pull up the hood on my jacket, determined to find something worth clicking the shutter for. I wander around the yard taking a few test shots: raindrops on the lawn swing, buds on the Virginia creeper—and then I see them. Lilac buds.

I remember the season when fading lilacs roused me from busyness to an awareness of time passing. I don't want to miss any more. *Shake it off, Linda.* Despite appearances and a head cold, it's spring. Soon fragrant purple lilac blossoms reminding everyone of their childhood and their mothers will burst forth in bloom. The garden will feed us as the days grow long and hot. This grey is nothing more than a temporary delay of the inevitable. Spring will win; it always does. I shift my focus from what isn't to what is right here in front of me. Lilac buds, and the gift of being un-busy enough to enjoy them. I make a pact with myself to extend lilac season by photographing these buds from now through the time when they're drying and dying.

I lean toward the bush and focus my macro lens on the promise of blossoms. What a gift, this time in which I can go half-dressed out into the yard and look for magic. I've focused on gratitude these past months and been intentional about noting small and simple things. In these still-tight buds I see promise; in the fading, falling blossoms months from now, chances are I will see something else. When the lilacs finish blooming and I realize the season didn't seem so brief this year, I will have moved from all-encompassing gratitude of the moment to wholistic adoration. I see God everywhere and in all things. It seems like an elementary fact of my faith, but I never saw it this way before. The closer I pay attention the clearer I see it. The magic in the garden, the way one thing in creation works together with another, the dark nights and the grey mornings, the inevitable promise of spring, and the synergy of it all: it's all testimony to the Creator who crafted it.

Chapter 12

ACCEPTABLE WORSHIP

*God has engrained in all of us particular passions, drives
and interests, and in pursuing them with a Godward
perspective, we engage in worship.*

Adam McHugh, *Introverts in the Church*

I wrestle through fear every week to facilitate a women's
Bible study. It's a stretch for me as an introvert, but my
desire to serve is more powerful than my wily adversary,
fear, so I push through my discomfort. One afternoon
we're gathered in the chilly basement of our church and I'm
sipping licorice tea from my thermos and thinking about
pulling on my jacket when someone offers the thought that
acceptable worship is anything offered in gratitude with
honour and wonder.

I think about it later in terms of the words I tap out every morning to contribute something edifying to the collective conversation. I try to draw the reader's attention to thin, often ordinary, places where the divine intersects with our days. I'm no scholar. I can't, and have no desire to, discuss or write about doctrine and theology, but I can write about the things I know for sure and stake my life on. Are these ordinary ruminations acceptable worship?

Author Rebecca Pippert advises, "Let God make you fully you. Rejoice in your God-given temperament and use it for God's purposes. This point cannot be emphasized enough. We must be authentic. If we try to be someone we are not, people will see it instantly."[78] Isn't that exactly what I learned in the great encounter? Adam McHugh, an introvert and kindred spirit, says, "Contemplatives know that God's voice rarely comes in thunder but rather in a whisper, creeping into the lives of shepherds in isolated settings or to prophets gasping in thin mountain air."[79] Or to women sitting behind closed French doors reading scripture, scribbling truth, and listening hard.

In ancient times, a man named Paul stood before a king called Agrippa and told about an experience and an encounter on a dusty road leading to a town called Damascus when his life's mission became clear: tell people you have seen me and tell them what I will show you in the future.[80] In other words, find fresh ways to tell timeless truth. How can I do anything but offer my own words as a holy sacrifice?

Love tells me my simple gift, offered in gratitude and wonder is enough—it's worship. My gift can be used even though I dropped it, the paper it's wrapped in is torn and tattered, and what's inside is broken. Love calls me accepted—beloved. Nothing will make me any more real and valuable than I already am.

You're enough, Daughter. I hear it whispered in the still, quiet place where true wisdom doesn't always align with the world's wisdom and, for the first time in a very long time, I rest in my position as a daughter. *Be still*, it says. Seek timeless truth and don't worry about the latest and greatest new-fangled philosophy. *Use the measure of what I've given you for the benefit of others.* It's just that simple.

Frederick Buechner, in reflecting on certainties in a life filled with uncertainty, considered the subject of his writing. It will never reach as wide an audience as he'd like, he supposed, because it's "too religious for secular readers . . . and too secular for religious ones."[81] Getting past the fear of writing it is one thing, thinking about who might read it is another. I counsel a writer to consider her audience and, as I do, think in terms of my own scribbling. Who am I writing for? Who cares about the thoughts of an almost sixty-year-old grandmother? I write first for my Creator but I'd be lying if I said I didn't hope someone else might read my work, find something in it to help them so they, in their own way, can help someone else. I write because it's what I've always done, because I believe it's my calling in this season, and as a daily offering of acceptable worship.

I've been a behind-the-scenes prayer partner for a group of women, and they invite me to gather with them one evening to talk about *Two Hearts*, writing, and how God forms something beautiful out of the messes we make. In the days leading up to it I worry about what I might say of any interest or value. I pray meeting flawed heart to flawed heart will be enough because I have little else to offer. I'm still stumbling my way along this rocky and precarious path with no clearer picture of my destination than when I started the journey. It's a one of provision for a day at a time.

The evening starts with butterflies, of course. Any time I go somewhere unfamiliar I get nervous, start second-guessing, and wonder if there's a way I can get out of it. I know these women, some better than others. They've read my book and know far more about me than I know about them. But even so, there are those butterflies. There's no need to pull on a mask before I head out into the cold December evening but I'm tempted to toss one in my bag in case I need it. Driving through the dark, I pray: *Less of me, more of you.*

I time my arrival carefully. I don't want to be too early or too late. I kick my shoes off at the door of a home I haven't been to before, not realizing I'm walking into the middle of something so beautiful. They're a small group of women of varying ages and experiences who gather week after week to grow in faith, get real, and walk together through this messy life. They sip tea and munch cookies in what looks like an ordinary living room but, really, it's church. It's love, and laughter flowing, prayers offered, and hearts opened in a safe and oh-so-sweet place. These women are blessed to do this together week after week. I think this was what Jesus had in mind. We talk about my story and their stories and we pray for one another like it's as natural as breathing, the way prayer is meant to be. My simple prayer, offered in nervousness as I drove, is answered beautifully as grace falls like a soft blanket.

"Can you tell us what your new book is about?" one woman asks toward the end of the evening.

I haven't said it aloud, but it feels safe to do so here in this holy place.

"Faith," I reply after a slight hesitation in which I consider whether speaking it aloud might jinx it or scare the muse away. "It's about my faith."

It is, and it isn't. The truth is I'm not sure what it's about because I'm still working it out and figuring out how to shape it into acceptable worship. For now, saying it's about faith is enough.

Before I know it, it's time to go home and—surprising to me—I'm not eager to leave. But I leave carrying a glow and feeling like I've spent the evening on holy ground because, of course, I have.

Someone tells me something, and it reminds me we don't understand the real stuff going on in one another's lives. I wish there was some rhyme or reason—some logic— behind the number of trials any one person is expected to weather. Why does it seem like some of us get through life relatively unscathed while others limp along bruised and broken? Mine is not the most wrenching of journeys, neither has it been the easiest. That's hardly the point. We've all got a measure, we all know what *sehnsucht* feels like, and we've all been eyes-wide-open in our beds at night asking for answers to big questions. We think an explanation will help us understand but none are forthcoming. I think if I hadn't lost my first maternal connection, I'd be stronger. It's absurd to believe God won't put loads on us we're not able to carry because he can, and he will, and he does. And in those darkest of times we learn to trust in our belovedness.

Another person tells me another something and I'm struck by her transparency. If I were in her position, I'd be inclined to hold it close. But the telling of this thing, which isn't really such a big thing (a thing large enough to occupy my thoughts for an entire afternoon, nonetheless) causes me to feel a closeness to the individual I didn't before. That's always been hard for me—transparency. I started erecting walls when I sensed the first loss and they've only grown taller and thicker over the years. The problem is the walls meant to keep me from hurting keep out the beautiful as well as the terrible. Most tragic of all, they kept me from hearing the still, small voice of love for so long.

I receive an email and there is something in it that makes me sad though that was not the sender's intent. My confession, in a previous email, that a melancholy had settled over me as heavy as the morning fog opened the door for this individual to confess her own morose feelings over a recent interaction. That she shares it blesses me and gives me an opportunity to pray for her. Transparency, vulnerability, constantly going and doing have robbed me of these simple, priceless things.

We're all fragile and everything can change in an instant. For years, I shied away from those who seem to have it all together, because I didn't. Then I learned that underneath the façade we're all broken. We're not all "tough cookies" (as a medical practitioner referred to me after a particularly uncomfortable procedure); some of us are puddles of spilled milk. There's something, sometime, that brings all of us to our knees. When I see you in your brokenness, I feel safe enough to reveal a bit of my own, and before you know it, we slip our masks aside and see each other real face to real face. It's a beautiful thing.

Chapter 13
LONG LOST FAMILY

Today, people are so disconnected that they feel they are blades of grass, but when they know who their grandparents and great-grandparents were, they become trees, they have roots, they can no longer be mowed down.

Maya Angelou

Absence was the first thing. As a full-term newborn baby, delivered with the help of forceps and then taken from her distraught and overwhelmed mother and thrust into a loud and confusing world with nothing and no one familiar to comfort her and quiet the cacophony, the absence of my mother's heart was the first thing I felt as I tried to make sense of this world. I like to think the foster mother who cared for me for the first three months was patient with a baby who "seldom cried." But maybe I bonded with her and her absence only cemented the belief already becoming deeply ingrained: there was something terribly wrong with me and I could trust no one.

According to my adoption file, when the caseworker placed me in the arms of my quiet, twenty-nine-year-old adoptive mom, Laura, as my beaming adoptive dad, Ed, looked on, I "looked lovely in a little blue dress." My "new parents were very pleased," and "the placement was comfortable and relaxed." In photographs taken that day, my wide eyes look shell-shocked. Ed and Laura were thrilled. I was, in all probability, wary.

They were told I was a blank slate, and still young enough to be molded. Social workers had matched the physical characteristics of my birth and adoptive parents and told them It would be as if I was their biological daughter. I would adapt. Everything from before—Mary, Frank, my heritage and genetic predisposition, the instability of my first months of life—was wiped away with the stroke of a pen on a legal form changing my name and family, and putting a seal of secrecy on my truth. But I was not a blank slate and *sehnsucht* had already become a part of who I was.

It's early evening toward the end of May. The appointment has been in the back of my mind all day with a mixture of both anticipation and nervousness. A few weeks ago,

I received an email from my cousin—Mary's brother's daughter, Ruth. We connected via email a few years ago, and subsequently spoke on the phone, but we've never met in person. She and her husband will be passing through Kamloops and she wondered if we might get together for coffee.

Gerry and I arrive early at the hotel where Ruth and her husband, Dick, are staying. I don't want to appear too eager and I don't want to be impolitely late, so we take a seat in the lobby to pass some time. My husband scrolls through photos on his phone, and I sit on the edge of my chair watching the clock. I estimate it will take about one minute to walk from the lobby to the dining room where we've arranged to meet, so at one minute before the appointed rendezvous time, I stand.

"Okay, let's go." I run my hands down my shirt to smooth out any wrinkles and straighten my stance trying to exude a confidence I don't feel.

I recognize Dick as soon as we enter the dining room (say what you will about the pitfalls of social media; it benefits family seekers like me). We make eye contact, and he smiles as he walks toward us.

"There's a face I recognize," I say, trying to keep the mood light.

But Dick has a twinkle in his eye and, as I will come to know, an easygoing and welcoming manner that quickly wipes away my anxiety. Ruth is behind him, a kind-faced, smiling woman, and there's something in her I recognize as family right away. I sense kindred spirits in both of them.

They tell us there has been some confusion: the tour bus they were on was late arriving and they're just now having dinner. No matter. We join them in their booth, order glasses of iced tea, and get to know one another.

Through photos she pulls out after she's finished her meal, Ruth introduces me to her siblings, Joyce and Ken (my cousins!), their children, and grandchildren. We talk about a little one who had heart surgery earlier in the day, who I prayed for this morning (my knowledge of the procedure, again, thanks to social media). We talk about Mary, her insecurities and difficulties, and I'm reassured the stable and loving home Ed and Laura provided was a gift.

When they've finished their meal, the server brings a dessert menu for Ruth and Dick. Gerry and I decide to share a decadent chocolate dessert too. I don't taste one bit of it. I'm never comfortable with people I've just met (I'm rarely comfortable with people I've known for a long time either, for that matter), so it's a sweet little miracle I feel completely at home with these two as we chat and get to know one another.

"I read your book and brought a list of questions I wanted to ask you," says Ruth. "But I left it in the room."

We laugh, and she remembers the important questions. I'm comfortable enough to ask a few too. Conversation turns to the early deaths of some of our family members.

"You're still so young," Ruth says.

But I don't see myself as young. I've had a sense of living on borrowed time since I turned fifty-five, the age Laura was when she died suddenly of a pulmonary embolism. It's only intensified since I turned fifty-nine, the age Mary was when she, too, died suddenly (coincidentally, also of a pulmonary embolism).

I lay part of the blame for my sense of morbidity at the feet of Mary's younger sister, Katie, who was the first person I connected with from my birth family when I was twenty-six years old. In the first letter I received from her she said: "I have one sister left from the family. We're the only two who have made it beyond our 60th birthdays. My mother, father, and brother all passed away before they reached 60." She didn't mention Mary died at age 59, too. "My mother was 47," she went on to say. "All had heart problems." Katie's handwritten introduction to the family cast a shadow over the rest of my life. (Eventually I do some family math and see things from a different perspective. Mary's older sister, Esther, a kind woman who welcomed me as family, lived to age 83. Katie herself lived to age 70. Cousin Ruth and her siblings, Joyce and Ken, broke the early-death mold too, and have remained strong, vibrant, and healthy.) I'm closing in on 60 and am cautiously optimistic I'll make it past the dreaded milestone.

The dining room is all but empty when we talk about wrapping up our time together for now. Ruth and Dick have an early start in the morning and it's long past the time Gerry and I typically turn in for the night. We talk of getting together again. Gerry and I have been tossing around the idea of a summer trip to Saskatchewan for my prairie fix. Now it's a given. On the way out of the restaurant, I ask a server to take a photo of the four of us. Amidst laughter, we say "Fifty-nine!" instead of "cheese!"

"I love them!" I whisper under my breath as Gerry and I walk toward our car.

I have trouble sleeping. I replay our conversation and bask in the gift of a cousin reunion, feeling blessed and a little bit melancholy. What would it have been like to have grown up with cousins? Or to live nearby and be able to drop by for coffee and a visit now and then. *Sehnsucht.* There it is again.

———————

I dub it the Long-Lost Family (LLF for short) vacation. Less than two months after the cousin-reunion with Ruth and Dick, Gerry and I are on the road heading toward Saskatchewan. Our itinerary will include first-time meeting and an overnight stay at the home of Ruth's sister, Joyce, in Swift Current, and an overnight stay with Ruth and Dick in Saskatoon. Bracketed by visits with our kids and grand-kids in Calgary and Prince George, and with a few days' respite in the middle of it all to "take the waters" at the Temple Gardens mineral spa in Moose Jaw, it's a dream-come-true trip for me.

We're driving across the prairie on a short leg of our LLF vacation and, as we cross the provincial border into

Saskatchewan, I convince Gerry to stop at the sign indicating we're now in the province I call my heart's home. I get giddy and silly and he takes photos of me leaping for joy next to the *Saskatchewan, Naturally* sign and poking up out of the sunroof of our Ford Escape with hands raised in celebration. There's nothing but big sky all around. A warm wind blows and the deepest part of me relaxes into the feeling of being home. We pile back in the car and carry on farther down the Trans Canada. I drink in prairie and Gerry comments on the melancholy of a grove of trees in the absence of a house or outbuildings. A few hours later, we're standing in such a place.

We've enjoyed a delicious and comfortable lunch at the home of my cousin, Joyce, and her husband, Ted, in Swift Current. Joyce and I have spoken on the phone and exchanged brief emails, but this is the first time we've come face-to-face. I worried about coming to stay with people I didn't know, but it turns out my fears were unfounded. I'm as comfortable with Joyce and Ted as I was with Ruth and Dick a few weeks earlier. Ted suggests a drive after lunch.

"Would you like to see the Letkeman farm?"

For years, after I learned the name of the village Mary's family was from, I felt a tug whenever I drove past the sign on the Trans Canada Highway. Every time I told myself the next time I'd turn off and travel side roads leading to— well, I didn't know exactly where. I had no clue what I'd see when I got there, or even what to look for. It seemed like a foolish whim so I never did it. So, yes. I would very much like to see the Letkeman farm.

We pile into Ted's vehicle—Mennonite style, we joke—with Gerry taking the front passenger seat next to Ted, and Joyce joining me in the back. I'm delighted with the arrangement, and the opportunity to get to chat with Joyce and get to know her better as we head out on dusty prairie roads. Our conversation flows easily and gently and I come to understand more about our family. Stories I've already heard, and snippets of things I've imagined are clarified; others remain murky as is the nature of things in most families. It feels almost normal.

Mary and her sister, Esther, returned infrequently to Saskatchewan after they married and moved to British Columbia. The connection to their Saskatchewan nieces and nephews was weakened as a result. Like Ruth, Joyce didn't know Mary had surrendered two daughters to adoption until I opened the Pandora's Box. Joyce and I speculate on how difficult it must have been for her. Somehow talking about all of this with Joyce softens my heart even more to what Mary must have endured.

We're standing at the top of a hill where a slight indentation in the earth is the only thing left to indicate there was once a house on this spot. All around it is green. A modern-day crop of lentils grows on land that once grew wheat. A grove of trees is a melancholy witness to what this place once was, and a memorial to the people who once called this land home. My people.

My Letkeman grandparents who farmed this land never knew I existed but, in a sense, I feel as though I've come home to them. Scientists have extracted DNA from caves where ancient civilizations once dwelled. Is it too far-fetched to believe something of my grandparents remains? And of Mary, who was born and raised here? Maybe the reunion I sought with her at the cemetery in Chilliwack is happening here, at the place of her birth, instead.

Our teeth and bones absorb the air and water we take into our bodies, and science can access this information and trace our geographical journey. Place becomes part of us so, in a sense, I've always carried Saskatchewan in me, even after Ed and Laura moved us to British Columbia when I was thirteen years old. I've always felt it. The endless prairie whispers to me of home even now, long after those I grew up with and called family are all gone. But this place is part of me in a deeper sense. Or maybe I am part of it. I feel connection reach up from the land and through time. I feel roots take hold.

To the untrained eye it's endless green prairie. To someone who understands the history I am beginning to piece together it's NE 4-14-6-W3, a place where wild horses once roamed. It is the land my grandfather, Jacob Letkeman, filed homestead papers on, the place where he brought my grandmother, Mary, whom he married in 1913, to live. They tethered cows and hobbled horses until Jacob had the resources to build a fence to contain them. He hand-dug a well and built a small wooden shack for them to live in. The building would one day be repurposed as a henhouse, then a pig barn, and finally moved elsewhere where it was ultimately consumed by fire. This is the land from which my grandparents, Jacob and Mary, watched the railway come in and elevators go up for the newly formed town of Kelstern—a place that remains as a sign on the Trans Canada Highway pointing the way to a town that no longer exists. (It's a good thing I never tried to find it by myself.)

It's the land where my grandparents raised four low-German–speaking Mennonite children: Jacob, Esther, Katie—and Mary. When my grandparents left the farm, it was passed to their son, Jacob, and he raised his family— my cousins, Ruth, Joyce, and Ken—here. Now, Joyce points toward the west, the direction in which she and her low-German speaking siblings ran across fields toward a school where they spoke only English. They are the same fields, and the same experience, as that of Mary and her siblings before them. The warm wind blows across the fields caressing the green lentils into gentle waves. I raise my phone to shoot a 360-degree video.

"Oh look, there's Joyce!" I pan past my laughing cousin who is taking a photo with her phone.

"Oh look, there's Ted!" more smiles.

"And Gerry."

I come full circle and put my phone down. I look out over the fields and imagine children laughing.

And Linda. Here is Linda. At last.

Ted drives a short way along gravel prairie roads, turning left, then right. We pass the site where the school once stood. All that's left is a tall set of wooden swings. The Mennonite Brethren Church is on the property next to it—a large, modern structure built next to the spot where the old church once stood. Joyce points out a pile of discarded debris in an area next to the church yard and tells me our eccentric Aunt Katie once lived there. In her letters to me, Katie said she lived on a hobby farm. Joyce sets the record straight: it was a small lot with a not-very-well-kept trailer on it.

We drive farther and Ted stops at the little Elim Mennonite Brethren cemetery. There we find the graves of our grandparents. Lichen covers the worn headstones making them hard to read. Ted goes back to the car and returns with a brush to clear them so we can take photographs. Here I am, standing at the graves of our grandparents with my cousin, like any other ordinary person. It is such a simple thing, but something that seemed impossible for much of my life. It is about as close to a perfect day as I can imagine.

I need a break after that. We arrive in Moose Jaw, the small city with a population of approximately 34,000 where I spent my childhood, around noon. We don't have to use the navigation system here. I easily direct Gerry to 1065 Seventh Avenue Northwest and the house Dad built before I was born—the house we lived in until, with my heart breaking, we moved to British Columbia.

It looks well-maintained and cared for, albeit smaller than it seemed when I was a child. I think of endless summer evenings spent playing tag with my friends in the front yard, and frigid Saturday winter afternoons skating on the rink Dad made by flooding the driveway. The garage where Dad parked his Oldsmobile looks the same—but also smaller. I remember the wall lined with license plates, the window looking into our neighbour's backyard, and how Mom and Dad scolded my sister and I when they caught us peeking through it. There's a pickup truck in the driveway.

"Why don't you knock on the door and tell them your dad built this house and ask if they'll let you look around?" Gerry suggests.

"No, no," I protest.

I imagine the interior is renovated and updated and bears little resemblance to the way it looked a half-century ago when we left. I've stood on Seventh Avenue in front of this house a handful of times as an adult, tempted to walk up the cement steps (not the original ones), knock on the door, and ask the same question. I hesitate because there's nothing left of what once was. The past remains only in my memories, and that is as it should be.

Gerry and I cross the street and walk toward the Minto United Church where I attended Sunday school. The footprint has changed but the blonde brick façade is the same. I try to identify the original part of the building and the Christian Education Centre where I attended Brownies and weekly choir practice. I point out houses where the Langstaffs, the Smalls, and the Montgomerys once lived. And the little house where a man named Henry sat at the window and watched the world go by.

We return to the Escape, and Gerry drives up the back alley where my friends and I made up adventures and ran free. He stops behind what was once our backyard. I point out the place where Dad parked our Scamper trailer, where mom tended a fire in the burning barrel, and where a maple tree with a branch I could sit on and be invisible grew. The little garage where Mom parked her Ford Falcon is still there. In the summer she left her car outside, and Debbie Green and I set up wooden crates and played school in it. We threw old blankets over the top of Dad's sawhorses in the shade next to it to make forts.

The Escape's tires crunch on the gravel as Gerry makes his way down the alley toward Oxford Street, turns left, then right, and heads down Seventh Avenue through Caribou

Street West to Moose Square and the house where Dad grew up. I take a few photos and we carry on with our tour.

We stop for an early supper, then walk through Crescent Park past the old library and the natatorium swimming pool, the places I frequented as a child, as Dad did before me. There's so much of my history in this small city. I'm rooted here too. It's different than the natural rooting I felt when I was standing on the Letkeman land. This is the place of my memories representing who I am by way of nurture. The connection is different, but no less real.

———————

The next morning, Gerry and I grab a coffee and go exploring—south, where it's flat as flat can be. The map on the navigation system shows nothing: no lines representing roads or railway tracks, no bodies of water or parks. Nothing. We're in the middle of nowhere. We drive gravel range roads and township roads with no specific destination in mind, passing falling-down barns, gaggles of shiny silver granaries, and groves of trees hiding farmhouses. But mostly there's nothing but wide-open prairie and large, living sky. It's the sweetest sight in the world. In the unobstructed view I see past, present, and possibility. I sense God's endless love.

Gerry pulls over to the side of the road and stops the car. I step out and the silence is loud in my ears as I breathe deep and slow in a way I don't anywhere else. Gravel crunches underfoot as I wander in contented awe.

The warm wind is a welcome embrace, the dusty smell is that of home. I pull out my camera and shoot images to feed me after we leave this place, pressing the shutter button again and again. We return to the car and set off, turning left, heading south; then right, heading east in the general direction of Highway 39, which will take us north back toward Moose Jaw so we can get something to eat and drink. We're in no hurry. For now, we drink prairie. It's more than satisfying.

––––––––––––––

"We've all read your book so we know all about you."

Oh my. That's not intimidating at all.

We spent the afternoon in Saskatoon with Ruth and Dick. We enjoyed lunch at their home, and a drive (Mennonite style) around the city and out to the bedroom community where they lived before moving to the city. Then we had a visit with their daughters, Carrie and Carla, and an afternoon treat—a first for Gerry and me—of delicious Mennonite *rollkuchen*. We talk about life, family, and food. I learn about *wareneki* and *schmauntfat* and other high-caloric but-if-they're-as-delicious-as-*rollkuchen*-worth-some-laps-around-the-neighbourhood-to-work-them-off-occasionally Mennonite favourites I resolve to try in the future. Now we've joined cousins of varying degrees in the back room of a restaurant reserved for a mini Letkeman reunion.

Gerry and I are given a place of honour in the middle of the table. It's a lot for an introverted girl like me. I'm a little overwhelmed but profoundly grateful to be here and for the connections. For the first time in my life I'm sitting in a room with a group of others who share my DNA. It's so normal. It's so extraordinary. We're laughing, telling stories, and talking about parents and grandparents and figuring out how we all fit together. It's the most precious thing.

I imagine secrets and shame coming into the light as we speak of things left too long, unspoken. I see frayed ends of broken threads weaving themselves together into something new. I think about Mary, and what she would think about all of this. I wish she could have known it would turn out okay. There's nothing to be done about what happened in the past except shine a light and honour those, like Mary, who were not treated with the dignity they deserved. It's good. It's right. And it's about time.

I ping-pong my head and take in the prairie as Gerry drives toward the mountains. If I drink in enough, maybe I'll sustain the sense of strength I feel here once we get home. It's more than the prairie making me feel strong, though. It's the gift of being welcomed into my family.

A few weeks before we left on our LLF vacation, I received an email from one of Gerry's cousins. We intended to see him and his wife in Calgary and I was bringing a copy of *Two Hearts* for one of his family members—a reunited adoptee. He wrote to remind me of the woman's name so I could inscribe the book.

"This is a good news story," he said in the email.

Her birth family welcomed her with open arms, and she has the support and love of her adoptive family. They say she now also has a "Manitoba family." I nodded when I read his words because my story was turning into a good news story, too. For years, when I spoke of my deep connection to Saskatchewan, inevitably someone would ask if I had family there.

"I have no family except for my children," I answered during the dark years.

It was too complicated to try to explain. My family-less status suited me for a time, granting me the gift of growing into myself on my own terms, but I never stopped missing Saskatchewan. In times of melancholy I wondered what it would have been like if we hadn't left and if everyone I loved hadn't died. Who would I be if I hadn't been alone? Now, as the LLF vacation winds down and we drive toward the mountains, my eyes linger on the prairie in the rear-view mirror and I think about that adoptee, her "good news story," and her "Manitoba family." After all these years I have a good news story of my own: I have a "Saskatchewan family."

———————

We take a drive one afternoon in mid-November because the sun is shining. Gerry steers along winding country roads, and we scan the sides and the distant hills for something photo worthy. Nothing interests us enough to stop.

"It's too bad the mountains are in the way of the view," I mutter.

My husband smiles, understanding my love for the wide-open prairie and how the mountains have always hemmed me in. The brilliant colours of autumn are gone, the season's finest, crisp and messy are on the ground. It's stick season. I hold my camera on my lap and play with tiny magnets in the thumb and index fingers of my gloves, flipping the end of each finger back and forth. The gloves were a gift from my team when I retired almost five years ago—a gift given tongue-in-cheek because we were moving back to the frozen Canadian north. They'll come in handy if I ever brave the sub-zero temperature to take photos. Maybe this will be the year.

We take a detour on the way home through a growing neighbourhood of too-big houses in too-small yards. They're such a contrast to the small, but comfortable house Dad built in Moose Jaw and the tiny house where my grandma, Belle, raised Laura and her siblings. The footprint of Belle's house was smaller than the attached garages in this neighbourhood. These places are behemoths. They sit empty most weekdays, cleaned and cared for by someone else because the adults who live here are busy, prosperous, and motivated. They are our future.

It's late Sunday afternoon, and I wonder if the gnawing has begun: that Sunday Night Feeling. The dread at the prospect of hopping back on the treadmill in the morning. I wonder if they've unplugged over the past two days or if they stayed engaged with the pulse of their chosen careers. I wonder if they'll look back on these as halcyon days or days of quiet desperation. I wonder how much bigger houses need to be.

We head toward home and a Yorkie waiting for her supper. I put her dish down in front of her and she dances and licks her chops as if it's the most delicious meal in the world instead of the same thing I've served every night for a decade. She digs in, and I go downstairs to survey my canning shelves and rummage in the freezer for inspiration for supper.

"I don't want to make dinner," I whine to Maya, who wolfed hers down as if she was starving and then followed me downstairs.

But I pull roasted tomatoes, green peppers, onions, basil, and garlic from the freezer and take them upstairs to make a sauce. Gerry's nose leads him upstairs from where he's been at his computer planning hikes and, as I'm tossing dried oregano snipped from the front yard a few months ago into the pot, he leans over for a closer look and wraps an arm around my waist.

"It sure smells good in here."

I stir and cook, he switches on the news, and there is a distinct absence of the Sunday Night Feeling that was the norm during my corporate years. Now there is gratitude, contentment, and, still, a gentle longing for home.

Chapter 14
SWEET LIFE

Your life is not something from which you can stand aside and consider what it would have been like had you had a different one. There is no "you" apart from your actual life. You are not separate from your life, and in that life you must find the goodness of God. Otherwise, you will not believe that he has done well by you, and you will not truly be at peace with him.

Dallas Willard, *The Divine Conspiracy*

In January Gerry and I take a vacation, returning to a resort in the Mayan Riviera we've been to before, to enjoy some "sweet life" I saw advertised on a billboard all those years ago. When we were still working, we looked forward to getting away from the mind-numbing busyness for a few weeks in the winter. In retirement, I want to craft a life we don't need a vacation from, but a respite from the Canadian winter is a blessing. It's been five years since I walked away from corporate-busy into another kind of busy. I understand the folly of seeking significance in accomplishments, have learned the wisdom of sitting still, and walked through a season of sweetness in which I found something I didn't know I was looking for. It's taken sixty years to get to the place where I believe in my belovedness. Maybe I'm a slow learner or maybe I've come to this truth at precisely the right time.

One morning, Gerry and I rise before dawn, grab our cameras, and head to the beach to photograph the sunrise. Sunrise is glorious anyplace but on a beach in the Mayan Riviera it is especially so. We stop at the bar where they're just opening up, for lattes, and by the time we get to the beach a handful of hopefuls have already gathered. Some stand with their toes in the ocean and others, like us, sit in silence on the edge of blue lounge chairs. I bury my toes in the sand and pray while we wait for a miracle—the genesis of a brand-new day.

The crescendo of waves plays the music of creation as the sun breaks over the horizon and we who have gathered to witness the miracle fall silent, struck by the majesty. I lift my camera, aware of the paradox between my relative physical smallness and the magnitude of my belovedness. My attention shifts from awe at the creation manifested in the sunrise to the Creator and, in the holy hush of dawn, I worship.

———————

I'm sitting in one of the resort lobbies enjoying another latte while Gerry is off on his morning walk. It's my sixtieth birthday. I exhaled when I woke up this morning with the thought that I've reached the age neither Mary nor Laura did. The resort is beautiful and relaxing, with opportunities for activities and excursions and, even here, a subtle push for more. It's easy to fall into the trap of busy. I create a sanctuary around my table with my coffee, notebook, pens, and books where I write, pray, reflect, and worship. I have church.

The older I get, the simpler it all seems: love God and love others, glorify the Creator and enjoy the creation. Yet, I'm still prone to tie myself up in knots trying to understand how it should play out. It would be enough if I could get a handle on how to love. I try, but on too many days I fail—before my feet hit the floor some days. I rely on mercy, trust in grace, and try again. Sometimes, I recite the *Shema* in my mind when the blanket of not-love falls over me. *Hear, O Israel, the Lord your God, the Lord is one.* Listen, Linda, to the most important thing the Creator asks of you. *Love the Lord your God with all your heart, and mind, and soul, and strength.* All encompassing, with everything you've got, living and active. It's as simple and as difficult as that. Honestly, I'm not sure what the loving God part looks like, but I keep trying to figure it out. I think I'm closer than I was five years ago but mostly it's two steps forward and one step back.

I remember the addendum added by God's only begotten: *And love your neighbour as yourself.* That neighbour part; that's the most challenging of all. Because people cut you off in traffic, have different opinions, and want to zig when I want to zag. Too often my first response isn't love.

If I could get a handle on what it means to love God and love people and do it consistently, I might come to the end of my days satisfied I had accomplished what I was called to do. I keep trying, failing, and getting up again. I remind myself that faith expressing itself through love is the only thing that counts, and that I'm called to write timeless truth for the benefit of others in this season. And I think about the sweetness.

––––––––––––––

A storm blows in one night, tossing palm branches and debris all over the manicured resort. Gerry and I are having dinner when it hits. We watch the torrential downpour and the whipping of palm fronds from the sanctuary of our table near the window. When we're finished our meal, we run from the lobby to our villa, ducking our heads against the wind to dodge raindrops, getting thoroughly soaked in the process.

In the morning, the air is fresh and the sun shines bright in the cloud-free sky. We pass ground maintenance workers on the way to breakfast. They are busy raking up dead leaves and branches liberated by the storm. I remember my dream about the raging storm absorbing all my pain as I wailed into it. I woke before the storm in my dream ended, but I imagine the air afterward must have been as clean and honest as this Caribbean morning.

It's cloudy, and not as warm as we'd like. Gerry and I are lying next to each another on deck chairs beside the adult pool in a quiet part of the resort. We came to escape the noise and busyness of families pushing children in strollers the size of small cars. An undercurrent of *something* has fallen on us. I don't know what precipitated it. A word spoken sharply in a certain tone, a misunderstood intention, something minor is stuck in our collective craw.

Nearby, a handful of others read, nap, and now and then swim across the pool and pad to the bar for a drink of something exotic. Other than an occasional soft-spoken remark shared between couples, it's quiet. It's cold-quiet under the umbrella where Gerry and I have set up for the afternoon. We focus on our books, but I've been on the same page for the past hour. The tension is distracting. We're disconnected and I'm not enjoying his presence. It must be like this with God when I'm too busy or overwhelmed to think about connection. I'm still in Divine presence, but I'm disconnected.

On a better day, when Gerry and I aren't at odds, we can be together by the pool or on the beach in much the same way we are this afternoon—absorbed in our books, napping or people watching, and all it takes is a word or a glance to rekindle our connection. When I consider serendipitous intersections in life that can only be orchestrated by a divine Maestro, or when I pause in the middle of something I've done a thousand times before to see the light playing on the hills, I remain mindful. When I take a close-up photograph of a flower opening to the sun, or lean into the gentle touch of a hand on my shoulder, take a moment to offer a silent one-word prayer—*thanks*—or, in dark times—*help*—I remain connected. The Divine is present in both my joy and in my grief. The sweetness taught me that.

Every morning, on our way to the beach to get a latte; and every afternoon, when we head back to our villa, sun-drunk and tired, to shower and change before dinner; we pass by an open-air church surrounded by palm trees in a manicured courtyard. *Nuestra Senora de las Nieves*. Our Lady of the Snows. From the yellow front façade rises a tall steeple-like structure. Two bells are visible through openings at the top, and a cactus in a terra cotta pot anchored on the corner reaches to the sky. Stands of fresh white flowers serve as greeters at the front entrance. The marble floor and polished wooden benches shine. Paintings of saints adorn the walls. A marble crucified Christ hangs on a crucifix at the front.

One morning, Gerry mentions the lanterns.

"What lanterns?" I ask.

He points out two massive cast-iron lanterns hanging on either side of the opening to the church. My attention has always been on the spire, the wooden pews, the phallic cactus, the bells, the paintings, or the smooth marble floors. I've never noticed the lanterns before. Gerry and I have looked at the same thing day after day but have seen something completely different.

We are a diverse people: beloved, every unique one of us. Some see the sum but miss individual parts, others focus on detail but miss the majesty of the whole. One worships in quiet contemplation, another in exuberant adoration. Some, in the majesty of a cathedral, others in an ordinary building, or simple open-air church like this. This person chews on deep theological truth; that one sees God in the simplicity of a leaf falling to the ground or a seed sprouting from the soil. We worship in the garden, with our feet in the sand, looking through the macro lens of a camera, or tapping out words of reflection and prayer. It doesn't have to look the same for all of us. We try to put God in a building or a box like a divine pet we visit now and then but he refuses to stay there. Deep calls to deep and we've no choice but to respond. It's not complicated but we're prone to make it so.

The presence I longed for came quietly. Unexpectedly. The sweetness that can neither be conjured nor contained left the same way. At first, I wondered if I had done something to cause it to go but now I see the gift was always meant to be fleeting. It lingers in the wind on the beach, in the shadows on the hills across the ridge at home, in the miracle of my garden, and in countless other ordinary extraordinary ways. The greatest gift—perhaps the reason for it all—was that my heart turned. I saw love in a way I hadn't before. I saw that it's always been about love.

Before Mary and Frank's pain came together, and Laura and Ed's joy was fulfilled when a social worker placed a squirming baby in a pretty blue dress in their arms; before the messes I made and even in spite of them, I was known and chosen. As were Mary and Frank and Laura and Ed and you, too. Sure, we mess up—none of us are as we wish all the time. We're broken and life's messy but there's still this unconditional, ineffable love whispering to us. I don't understand it but I believe it with every fibre of my being.

I'm still thinking about the lanterns as we walk away from the church toward the dining room. Gerry lets go of my hand and steps to the side so another couple can pass by. We smile in greeting—*hola!*—and continue on our way. I wonder if they'll see the lanterns, the cactus, or if they focus on something else altogether.

In a few days we'll fly home, back to the middle of a Canadian winter. It will be white and cold, and I'll look at images of the Caribbean sunrise to remind me of the sanctuary of this place. Memories fade. They grow softer around the edges. I suppose it's why we're drawn to capture them with photographs to try to hold on to them.

The time will come when my memories of the season of sweetness I experienced will grow dim too. I'll carry the sense that something profound happened, but I'll forget the fine details. I'll remember when I realized mind-numbing busyness wasn't serving me well, and I slowed down and heard a still, small voice whisper *beloved* to me.

As I work through the sweet torture of writing this book, I return again and again in my mind to that season, and yet the truth I came to understand so profoundly still slips from my mind and I find myself in the whirlpool of doing again. I live there for a while until I get tied up in knots and remember I hear wisdom the loudest in silence and solitude. I withdraw and listen, and there it is. That same sweetness—the same, only different because I'm different now and my need is not the same.

I didn't know I needed an experience, but an experience was what I got. It changed the substance and depth of my faith forever. The sweetness taught me God is always present but doesn't compete for my attention. I'm granted the freedom to run and seek significance elsewhere, but when I remember and return, there it is. That whisper. *Beloved.*

EPILOGUE

It's a wet and foggy morning in mid-November. Soon it will be winter but for now we live in the in-between. The snow that surprised us two days ago is all but gone. The pine trees on the other side of the fence stand melancholy, wrapped in clouds so thick I can't see the ridge across the valley at all. I stand at my bedroom window watching the fog do nothing but hover and think it is the wisest of all the things that jostle for my attention. I'm close to tears.

Three weeks ago, I had surgery. In the weeks leading up to it I was forced to slow down. I rested and felt my*self* return. Then I was hospitalized, the thing that needed to be tended to was, and I came home, minus a few parts, to rest and allow my broken body to heal. Every part of me is still recovering. I have occupied myself in the past couple of weeks editing and revising sections of this book and in the company of other good books. Gerry has taken me for drives and short shopping trips. A couple of times I've had coffee with a friend. Gradually, I've started to dip my toe back in real life. I am getting stronger, but I am not yet strong enough.

One afternoon, I hit a wall. After days of appointments, coffee and conversation, and trips to the grocery store, I felt myself shut down. My body ached and my mind felt overstimulated. I slipped easily back into believing I had to do something, that losing myself in a book for a couple of hours to allow my body to heal was unproductive. I began to feel guilty for needing more rest. I started comparing myself to others. I keep forgetting we're individuals.

The copious amount of quiet I need to maintain my balance could be too much for someone else—as the constant stimulation that fuels someone else would over-whelm me. Busy at forty doesn't look like it does at sixty. There are seasons to push through and others to pull back. My body and mind need time to heal. Wisdom shows me the difference. Ah, but there's the rub; I can't hear wisdom's whisper when I'm busy.

There is a saying—I've always attributed it to the 1970s television show, Kung Fu, but a quick consultation with my friend Google tells me I'm incorrect—that says something along the lines of when the student is ready, the teacher will appear. With the (forced) opportunity to stay home and read deep, I come across new writers I want to get to know and books I want to read. Online book ordering is my recuperation buddy.

I've long appreciated the wisdom of gentle and wise Henri Nouwen, and one day come across a title—*The Life of the Beloved*—that piques my curiosity. It aligns with the story I've been trying to tell. Maybe I'll find another facet of timeless wisdom in its pages, so I order it.

On the evening of the day it arrives, I crawl into bed at an embarrassingly early hour and reach for the book. There, in the hush of the evening of the day when the first snowfall of the season made the world white here, I find this wisdom:

"From all eternity, long before you were born and became a part of history, you existed in God's heart. Long before your parents admired you or your friends acknowledged your gifts or your teachers, colleagues, and employers encouraged you, you were already 'chosen.' The eyes of love had seen you as precious, as of infinite beauty, as of eternal value. When love chooses, it chooses with a perfect sensitivity for the unique beauty of the chosen one, and it chooses without making anyone else feel excluded."[82]

I struggled with whether to use the word "chosen" in this book. The love that poured over me that morning when I saw the truth of having been chosen redefined the word for me. I wrestled with how to explain it. In some drafts of this manuscript I took it out completely. In the end I decided I'd do my best to convey the precious inclusiveness of the word and trust you would understand my intent. Henri seems to have struggled likewise. "I wouldn't be surprised if a part of you protests against the idea of being chosen,"[83] he writes. "Still, I do believe deeply that . . . we have to claim for ourselves that we are . . . 'chosen.'"[84] In other words: "as the Beloved . . . we have been seen by God from all eternity and seen as unique, special, precious beings."[85] And: "The great joy of being chosen: the discovery that others are chosen as well."[86] Yes. That's exactly what I experienced that spring morning.

"Long before any human being saw us, we are seen by God's loving eyes. Long before anyone heard us cry or laugh, we are heard by our God who is all ears for us. Long before any person spoke to us in this world, we are spoken to by the voice of eternal love. Our preciousness, uniqueness, and individuality are not given to us by those who meet us in clock time—our brief chronological existence—but by the One who has chosen us with an everlasting love, a love that existed from all eternity and will last through all eternity."[87]

There's nothing more I can add. This is what being chosen means. It sums up the state of the beloved. This is the wisdom I need to help me remember I don't need to medicate myself with busyness or anything else to fix my brokenness. Maybe it's what you need to hear, too. This is the timeless truth I pray I've found a fresh way to tell in these pages.

ACKNOWLEDGEMENTS

With gratitude to Ed Cyzewski for developmental editing, Heather Stuart for copyediting, and Yvonne Parks for the beautiful cover and interior design. Also to the community of writers who inspire me to keep scribbling even when I want to stop.

Most of all, thank you to my husband, Gerry. I think you cringed when I told you I was writing another book, but you did your best to understand I'd gone slightly mad and gave me the gift of time to hole up with words through draft after draft. I love you seven.

SUGGESTED READING

Following is a far-from-comprehensive list of books that are my gentle companions. Some reflect on the craft of writing; others guide the reader in a spiritual direction of sitting still. Some do both; others do neither. I suggest you choose one or more to read and see where it takes you.

All is Grace: A Ragamuffin Memoir by Brennan Manning and John Blasé

Between the Dreaming and the Coming True: The Road Home to God by Robert Benson

Common Prayer: A Liturgy for Ordinary Radicals by Shane Claiborne, Jonathan Wilson-Hartgtove, and Enuma Okoro

Dancing on the Head of a Pen: The Practice of a Writing Life by Robert Benson

The Divine Conspiracy: Rediscovering Our Hidden Life in God by Dallas Willard

Flee, Be Silent, Pray: Ancient Prayers for Anxious Christians by Ed Cyzewski

Imitation of Christ by Thomas à Kempis

In Constant Prayer (Ancient Practices Series) by Robert Benson

Introverts in the Church: Finding our Place in an Extroverted Culture by Adam McHugh

The Jesus Creed: Loving God, Loving Others by Scot McKnight

Leaving Church: A Memoir of Faith by Barbara Brown Taylor

Life of the Beloved by Henri J.M. Nouwen

Praying with the Church: Following Jesus Daily, Hourly, Today by Scot McKnight

The Remarkable Ordinary: How to Stop, Look, and Listen to Life by Frederick Buechner

The Shack by Wm. Paul Young

Walking on Water: Reflections on Faith and Art by Madeleine L'Engle

The Writing Life by Annie Dillard

ABOUT THE AUTHOR

Linda Hoye lives in British Columbia, Canada with her husband and their doted-upon Yorkshire Terrier but will always be a Saskatchewan prairie girl. She is the author of *The Presence of Absence: A Story About Busyness, Brokenness, and Being Beloved* and *Two Hearts: An Adoptee's Journey Through Grief to Gratitude*. Find her online at www.lindahoye.com where she ponders ordinary days and the thin places where faith intersects.

Connect with her at:
Email: linda@lindahoye.com
Blog: www.lindahoye.com
Facebook: www.facebook.com/LindaHoyeWriter/
Instagram: www.instagram.com/lindahoye/

If you enjoyed this book, please consider posting a short review on your favourite book-related site. Reviews are gold to authors as they increase the visibility of our book so readers can find it. Thank you.

ENDNOTES

CHAPTER 1: SEARCHING

1 The verbiage in this section is taken directly from documents contained in my adoption file.

CHAPTER 2: MIND-NUMBING

2 The reference to Quadrant 1 and Quadrant 2 comes from Stephen Covey's Time Management Matrix in *The 7 Habits of Highly Effective People* (New York: Simon & Schuster, 1989). Quadrant 1 items are crises, pressing problems, and deadline-driven projects viewed as both important and urgent. Quadrant 2 items are relationship building and strategic planning—that which is important but not urgent. Covey says effective people focus most of their efforts in Quadrant 2.

CHAPTER 4: DARK NIGHT

3 C.S. Lewis, *The Problem of Pain*, (New York: HarperCollins, 1996), 161.

4   Henry Wadsworth Longfellow, *Hyperion,* (2004). Project Gutenberg. Retrieved November 20, 2019, from https://www.gutenberg.org/files/5436/5436-h/5436-h.htm.

5   Ibid.

6   Thomas à Kempis, *The Imitation of Christ* (n.p.: Enhanced Media Publishing, 2017), Kindle edition, 75.

7   Ibid., 85.

8   Ibid., 130.

9   Ibid., 380.

10   Ibid., 146.

11   C.S. Lewis, *Mere Christianity* (Los Angeles, CA: Green Light, 2014), Kindle edition, 32.

12   Ibid.

13   Henri Nouwen, *The Spiritual Life: Eight Essential Titles. The Way of the Heart: The Spirituality of the Desert Fathers and Mothers* (NewYork.: HarperOne, 2016), Kindle edition, 933.

14   Ibid.

15   Henri Nouwen, *Here and Now* (n.p. The Crossroad Publishing Company: 1994), Kindle edition, 28.

16   Ibid.

17   Carmen, Acevedo Butcher, ed., *The Cloud of Unkno*wing (Boulder, CO: Shambala Publications, 2009), 12.

18   Ibid.

19   Ibid.

20   Butcher, ed., *The Cloud of Unknowing*, 11.

21   Sarah Ruden, ed., *Confessions* (New York: The Modern Library, 2017), Kindle edition, 3.

CHAPTER 5: FEAR AND FAITH

22 Robert Benson, *Between the Dreaming and the Coming True: The Road Home to God* (San Francisco: HarperSanFrancisco, 1996), Kindle edition, 716.

23 Anne Lamott, in *Bird by Bird*, describes the first draft this way.

CHAPTER 6: CHOSEN

24 John Steinbeck, *Tortilla Flat* (1935; repr., New York: Penguin Group [USA], Inc., 2008), Chapter 4.

25 1 Peter 1:2, NLT.

CHAPTER 7: ONCE YOU ARE REAL

26 Verbiage taken from my adoption file.

27 The dialogue that follows is taken directly from court transcripts in my adoption file.

28 Margery Williams, *The Velveteen Rabbit* (Garden City, NY: Doubleday & Company, Inc.: 2004). Project Gutenberg. Retrieved December 18, 2019 from http://www.gutenberg.org/cache/epub/11757/pg11757.txt.

29 Ibid.

30 Brennan Manning, *Abba's Child: The Cry of the Heart for Intimate Belonging* (1994; repr., Colorado Springs, CO.: NavPress, 2015), 33.

31 John Eagan, *A Traveler Toward the Dawn: The Spiritual Journey of John Eagan* (Chicago: Loyola University Press, 1990), 150–151.

32 Ibid.

CHAPTER 8: DELIGHTS

33 Norman Wirzba, *Living the Sabbath: Discovering the Rhythms of Rest and Delight* (Grand Rapids, MI: Brazos Press, 2006), 12.

34 Ibid.

35 Ibid.

CHAPTER 9: SATURATING

36 Paraphrase from the *Book of Common Prayer* (TEC, 1979). pdf/137.

37 Ibid.

38 C.S. Lewis, *Mere Christianity*, 197.

39 Madeleine L'Engle, *The Crosswicks Journals: A Circle of Quiet* (New York: Open Road Media, 2017.), Kindle edition, 386–398.

40 Ibid., 398.

41 Gabor Mate, *In the Realm of Hungry Ghosts: Close Encounters with Addiction* (Toronto: Vintage Canada, 2008), 110.

42 The thought comes from fifteenth century Julian of Norwich, who lived the bulk of her life in seclusion in a church in Norwich, England. The most famous quote from her *Revelations of Divine Love* is "All shall be well, and all shall be well. And all manner of things shall be well."

CHAPTER 10: FALLOW

43 Isabel Allende, "How to Live Passionately—no matter your age," filmed in March 2014 at Whistler, British Columbia.

TED video, 8:09. https://www.ted.com/talks/isabel_allende_how_to_live_passionately_no_matter_your_age.

44 Ibid.

45 Ibid.

46 Madeleine L'Engle, *Walking on Water* (n.p.: Crosswicks, Ltd, 2001), Kindle edition, 188.

47 C.S. Lewis, *The Weight of Glory* (New York: Macmillan and Co., 1966), 4-5.

48 Ibid.

49 Madeleine L'Engle, *The Crosswicks Journals*, 386–398.

50 Thomas à Kempis, *The Imitation of Christ*, 2.

51 Ibid.

52 Ibid., 3.

53 Dictionary.com, *Collins English Dictionary – Complete and Unabridged* (2012 Digital Edition), https://www.dictionary.com/browse/fallowing.

54 Lucy Maud Montgomery, *Anne's House of Dreams*. (1996). Project Gutenberg. Retrieved December 18, 2019 from http://www.gutenberg.org/files/544/544-h/544-h.htm.

CHAPTER 11: DREAMING

55 C. S. Lewis, *Narrative Poems*, Preface to *Dymer* [1950], para. 5.

56 Madeleine L'Engle, *The Rock That Is Higher: Story as Truth* (1993; repr., Colorado Springs, CO.: Waterbrook Press, 2002), 17.

57 Ibid.

58 Kate Bowler, *Everything Happens for a Reason: And Other Lies I've Loved* (New York: Random House, 2018), Kindle edition, 121.

59 Ibid.

60 Ibid.

61 Martin Luther, *Exposition on the Lord's Prayer*, (London, 1844).

62 Ibid.

63 Wendell Berry, *Jayber Crow*, (Washington, DC: Counterpoint, 2000), Kindle edition, 51.

64 Ibid.

65 Sarah Bessey, *Miracles and Other Reasonable Things: A Story of Unlearning and Relearning God*, (Howard Books: 2019), 143.

66 Henri Nouwen, "Moving from Solitude to Community to Ministry," *Leadership Journal*, Spring 1995.

67 Ibid.

68 Ibid.

69 Ibid.

70 Isaiah 30:15.

71 Augustine, *Confessions*, translated by Henry Chadwick (Oxford: University Press, 2009), 132.

72 Wm. Paul Young, *The Shack* (Los Angeles: Windblown Books, 2007).

73 May Sarton, *Journal of a Solitude* (1972; repr., New York: Norton, 1992), 11.

74 Lucy Maud Montgomery, *The Story Girl* (New York, 1922; Project Gutenberg, 2004), http://www.gutenberg.org/files/5342/5342-h/5342-h.htm.

75 Ibid.

76 C.S Lewis, *The Four Loves* (London, 1960), Project Gutenberg, 2014, https://gutenberg.ca/ebooks/lewiscs-fourloves/lewiscs-fourloves-00-h.html.
77 Ibid.

CHAPTER 12: ACCEPTABLE WORSHIP

78 Rebecca Manley Pippert, *Out of the Saltshaker and Into the World*, (Downers Grove, Ill: InterVarsity Press, 1999), 110–11.
79 Adam McHugh, *Introverts in the Church: Finding Our Place in an Extroverted Culture* (Downers Grove, Ill: Intervarsity Press, 2009), Kindle edition, 1061.
80 Acts 26:16, NLT.
81 Frederick Buechner, *Now and Then* (New York: Harper, 1983), 108.

EPILOGUE

82 Henri J.M. Nouwen, *Life of the Beloved: Spiritual Living in a Secular World* (New York: Crossroad. 1992) 53–54.
83 Ibid., p 53.
84 Ibid.
85 Ibid.
86 Ibid., p 63.
87 Ibid., p 58.

CPSIA information can be obtained
at www.ICGtesting.com
Printed in the USA
LVHW111943070420
652571LV00001B/3

9 780993 730306